# Encouraging Words Regarding *Living Life on Purpose*

*"Living Life on Purpose* provides solid biblical teaching for recognizing all of life as sacred. This book points us beyond our self-centered agendas to embrace what God is doing in the world."

Dr. Bill Couch
Senior Pastor
Lakeridge United Methodist Church, Lubbock, Texas

"It is a serious decision in these days to take a stand for Jesus Christ. *Living Life on Purpose* encourages us to live our lives in a manner which reflects both awareness of what Christ has done for us and confidence based on what He has promised to continue to do in and through us."

David Long
President
OMS International, Inc.

"Maxie Dunnam has had a lifelong love affair with the church. In his service to the church as a Christ follower, he's been wholeheartedly committed to the cause of raising up Christian leaders to insure the integrity, faithfulness, and effectiveness of the church in reaching new generations for Christ. This book is a welcome resource both honoring Maxie and contributing to the great need for leaders of the future!"

Rev. Stephen Ramsdell
Senior Pastor
First United Methodist Church, Waco, Texas

"In a world that gets distracted trying to make a living, this book helps people know how to make a life. It speaks to people's hearts as well as their minds about things of eternal significance."

Dale Galloway
Founder and Director
The Beeson Institute, Asbury Theological Seminary

"This collection is a fitting tribute to Dr. Dunnam as it includes so many of the attributes of his long and fruitful ministry—thoughtful biblical applica-tion, solid ethics, good storytelling, and a down-to-earth tone. A good read for pastors and laypersons alike as they consider their own calling and encourage others to 'press on to take hold of that for which Christ Jesus took hold of [them]'."

Evie Telfer
Director of Campus Ministry
Messiah College

"My baby-boomer generation has enjoyed material success like no other generation. However, we are having to come to grips with the realization that true wealth is not in material possessions, but in the currency of heaven: the eternal destiny of people. These essays help us focus the rest of our days on earth towards our highest calling: being God's kingdom-minded people."

William M. Johnson
Entrepreneur
Canton, Georgia

"God can use these rich, understandable, and informed essays to reveal the universal—usually hard to define—longing which lies within all those who hunger to journey with Jesus. It is a longing to know God's calling and, perhaps, to possess the courage necessary to leave their comfort zones, security, and worldly identities to discover it and to live it out."

Don Mowat
Entrepreneur
Seattle, Washington

# Living Life on Purpose

# Living Life on Purpose

## THE JOY OF DISCOVERING
## AND FOLLOWING GOD'S CALL

Edited by
Maxie D. Dunnam and Steve G. W. Moore

Providence House Publishers
PROVIDENCE PUBLISHING CORPORATION
FRANKLIN, TENNESSEE

Printed in the United States of America

09       08       07       06       05       1       2       3       4       5

Library of Congress Control Number: 2005908770

ISBN-13: 978-1-57736-338-5
ISBN-10: 1-57736-338-8

*Cover design by Joey McNair*

PROVIDENCE HOUSE PUBLISHERS
an imprint of
Providence Publishing Corporation
238 Seaboard Lane • Franklin, Tennessee 37067
www.providence-publishing.com
800-321-5692

# CONTENTS

# FOREWORD

One of the special privileges for any board of trustees is when it gets to express appreciation to one of its leaders for service well done. As the chair of the Board of Trustees of Asbury Theological Seminary, I am privileged to dedicate this volume in honor of Dr. Maxie Dunnam in recognition of his ten years of service as the institution's president.

This volume and its companion volume, *A Thoughtful Faith* (Abingdon Press), were originally conceived of as a book that would pay tribute to Dr. Dunnam, currently chancellor of Asbury. But he would have none of it. In keeping with what has become his life's mission, Dr. Dunnam gave this space to focus on contributing to the work of the kingdom. Throughout his life as a pastor, denominational leader, and educational leader, Dr. Dunnam has faithfully sought to inspire and encourage anyone who would listen to love God more deeply and to follow Him more nearly.

Under his leadership, Asbury Theological Seminary has grown in the number of students it serves, launched campuses in Florida and on the World Wide Web, and reached out to serve the world in new and creative ways. These two volumes are a part of the heartbeat of what Asbury has been about for over eighty years: helping individuals discern and prepare for their calling as ministry leaders and cultivating a faith that unites and nurtures both head and heart. It is our hope and prayer that *Living Life on Purpose* and *A Thoughtful Faith* will extend the ministry of Asbury and also honor this special individual who has served so well.

James Smith
Chairperson of the Board of Trustees
Asbury Theological Seminary
2005

# ACKNOWLEDGMENTS

There are many people who deserve to be thanked for helping to make this volume possible. First and foremost are the Board of Trustees of Asbury Theological Seminary. They wisely saw the importance of honoring Dr. Maxie Dunnam for his years of service to Asbury as its fifth president. There are leaders who talk about grace and then there are those who live it out in all they do. Maxie Dunnam is one who lives it out. Anyone who has come to know him knows that he is a man passionately committed to being an agent of grace in the world in which we live. Nowhere is that more evident than in his desire to see people live their lives as a calling. This book is an expression of honor, but it is also an attempt to encourage and inspire everyone seeking to live out their faith from a sense of vocation and call.

Behind the scenes a number of people have worked editing, typing, researching, and proofreading. Kevin Dean, Sheila Lovell, Joseph Nader, and Scott Stockton have been of invaluable help. Harry Zeiders deserves special recognition as the all-purpose project support and faithful laborer. We are indebted to the people at Providence Publishing Corporation who took the original idea and helped us flesh it out in ways that would both honor Dr. Dunnam and serve to advance the work of Asbury and of God's kingdom. Of special help have been Andrew B. Miller and Nancy Wise, who have patiently and persistently kept us moving ahead in spite of numerous distractions and obstacles.

There were other individuals who were a constant source of encouragement and perspective. Included would be Paul and Jane Baddour, J. D. and Tiffany Walt, Elroy and Vicki Wisian, and, of course, Thanne Moore and Jerry Dunnam.

Our prayer would be that those who read this volume would have more of a sense of God's call upon their lives and a better understanding of how to follow that calling.

Steve G. W. Moore
Fall 2005

# CONTRIBUTORS

Bill Arnold (Ph.D.—Hebrew Union College) has sensed God's calling to be a pastor and an equipper of pastors. Arnold is professor of Old Testament and Semitic languages at Asbury Theological Seminary. He previously taught at Ashland Theological Seminary and Wesley Biblical Seminary. Among Arnold's recent volumes are *Dictionary of the Old Testament: Historical Books* (with H. G. M. Williamson), *Who Were the Babylonians?* and *A Guide to Biblical Hebrew Syntax*, written with John Choi.

Burrell Dinkins (Th.D.—Emory) has followed God's calling throughout the western hemisphere. With deep expertise in pastoral care and counseling, he most recently has served as the Johnson professor of pastoral leadership at the Dunnam Campus of Asbury Theological Seminary in Florida. In addition to pastoring and teaching in South America and the United States, Dinkins pioneered a clinical chaplaincy program for hospitals in Brazil.

Maxie Dunnam (Th.M.—Emory; D.Div.—Asbury Theological Seminary) has followed God's calling to pastor congregations, to be a catalyst for orthodoxy in the United Methodist Church, and to serve at the helm of one of the largest seminaries in the world. Dunnam is the chancellor of Asbury Theological Seminary and formerly led the seminary as its fifth president from 1994 to 2004. Before coming to lead Asbury, he served thriving pastoral charges at Christ United Methodist Church in Memphis, Tennessee, and elsewhere. Dunnam has been an active executive in the United Methodist Church, the World Methodist Council, and the Association of Theological Schools. His popular collections of writings include *The Workbook of Living Prayer, Unless We Pray*, and *Let Me Say That Again*. Among his recent titles is *A Thoughtful Faith*, edited with Steve G. W. Moore.

Ellsworth Kalas (B.D.—Garrett; D.Div.—Asbury Theological Seminary) has faithfully used his gifts and talents for more than fifty years as a preacher's preacher and as a teacher of preachers. Kalas currently serves as interim dean of the Beeson International Center for Biblical Preaching and Church Leadership, which provides cutting-edge education to select doctor of ministry students. His helpful books include *More Parables from the Backside* and *Grace in a Tree Stump*.

Chris Kiesling (Ph.D.—Texas Tech University) has served as a pastor, a campus minister, and, currently, as a seminary professor. He teaches courses in human development, discipleship, and campus ministry. Kiesling is widely sought after by students as a mentor and advisor. He is currently working on research in young adult development and spiritual formation.

Steve G. W. Moore (Ph.D.—University of Michigan) has served God as a campus minister, a professor, and a leader in Christian higher education. Moore is senior vice president of Asbury Theological Seminary, president of the Asbury Foundation for Theological Education, and professor of Christian leadership and discipleship. He is a popular speaker and a well-known leader in the fields of higher education, campus ministry, leadership studies, and board development. He has previously served as a vice president at both Seattle Pacific University and Baylor University. Moore's most recent book is *A Thoughtful Faith*, edited with Maxie Dunnam. His forthcoming works include *College 101: A Guide to Getting the Most Out of College* and *The Legacy Project: Presidential Leadership in Christian Higher Education*.

Sandra Richter (Ph.D.—Harvard) has been a part of the movement of God as a scholar of the ancient Near East. Richter is associate professor of Old Testament at Asbury Theological Seminary. She has taught at Harvard University, Harvard Divinity School, and Gordon-Conwell, and has also been active in parish ministry, Campus Crusade for Christ, and L'Abri Fellowship. Richter's scholarship has included numerous archaeological excavations and paper presentations at professional conferences.

# WALK WORTHY OF YOUR CALLING

*Maxie D. Dunnam*

IN THE WORLD TO COME, I SHALL NOT BE ASKED, "WHY WERE YOU
NOT MOSES?" I SHALL BE ASKED, "WHY WERE YOU NOT ZUSYA?"
—RABBI ZUSYA

I once heard a bishop tell of going to a church one Sunday morning to preach. He arrived early and decided that he would go to the Sunday school simply to see what was happening. When the bishop entered and took a seat in the back row, a little girl about nine years old stood up to give a recitation about characters in the Old Testament. When she came to Enoch, she said something the bishop never forgot: "Enoch was such a close friend of God that one day they took a walk together, and Enoch never came back."

## Enoch Never Came Back

Is there a better way to describe Enoch? The little that we have about him in Scripture doesn't tell us very much. We know that he was the son of Cain who had killed Enoch's uncle Abel.

Cain was so proud of his son that he built a city and named it after him. When Enoch grew up, of course, he married and had children. The seemingly distinctive detail about him as it relates to family was that when he was sixty-five years old, he became the father of Methuselah whom we know as the oldest man ever to live. Then Scripture says, "Enoch walked with God; then he was no more, because God took him away" (Gen. 5:24 NIV).

I like the way that young girl described Enoch: He "was such a close friend of God that one day they took a walk together, and Enoch never came back." That's beautiful.

The *walk* (i.e., walking with the Lord) is a common image in Scripture. Jesus Himself used the image over and over again. He issued the call, "follow me." When He wanted to define the meaning of discipleship, He expressed it very clearly: "If anyone would come after me, he must deny himself and take up his cross and follow me" (Matt. 16:24 NIV).

Remember the story of the rich young ruler who came to Jesus asking what he must do to inherit eternal life? After Jesus told him to keep all the commandments, the ruler responded that he had kept all the commandments since his youth. But Jesus observed, "You still lack one thing. Sell everything you have and give to the poor, and you will have treasure in heaven. Then come, follow me" (Luke 18:22 NIV).

Recall, as well, Jesus' beautiful declaration of being the Good Shepherd:

> . . . the sheep listen to his voice. He calls his own sheep by name and leads them out. When he has brought out all his own, he goes on ahead of them, and his sheep follow him because they know his voice. But they will never follow a stranger; in fact, they will run away from him because they do not recognize a stranger's voice. (John 10:3–5 NIV)

William Barclay's commentary on this passage includes a scene from a cave near Bethlehem:

Two shepherds had sheltered their flocks in the cave during the night. How were the flocks to be sorted out? One of the shepherds stood some distance away and gave this peculiar call which only his own sheep knew, and soon his whole flock had run to him, because they knew his voice. They would have come for no one else, but they knew the call of their own shepherd.[1]

So the call of Christ was for us to follow Him—to walk in His path, to walk in His way.

For Paul—not to mention most of the biblical authors in the Old and New Testaments—*walking* is a dominant metaphor and very important term. In Ephesians he uses this image at least seven times. A few of these passages are (according to the New American Standard Bible): "For we are His workmanship, created in Christ Jesus for good works, which God prepared beforehand so that we would walk in them" (Eph. 2:10). "Walk in love, just as Christ also loved you and gave Himself up for us" (5:2). "For you were formerly darkness, but now you are Light in the Lord; walk as children of Light" (5:8).

Beyond Ephesians, Paul uses this image repeatedly throughout his letters. Colossians 1:10 (NASB): "Walk in a manner worthy of the Lord." Romans 13:13 (NASB): "Let us behave [i.e., walk] properly as in the day." Second Corinthians 5:7 (NASB): "For we walk by faith, not by sight."

## Everything Is Grace

In Romans, chapter 6 verse 4, we read, "[W]e have been buried with Him through baptism into death, so that as Christ was raised from the dead through the glory of the Father, so we too might walk in newness of life." In the first five chapters of Romans, Paul has given us his reasoning about the doctrine of justification by grace through faith. We have absolutely nothing for which to boast, and we can do nothing to receive the favor of God. Only through faith can we see what God has given us. Everything is grace.

One day a woman spoke up in a Bible study class I was leading. I had been talking about grace and the saving work of Jesus Christ. She said, "You mean there is nothing I can do to save myself?"

"Absolutely nothing," I said.

With a lot of unbelief and almost desperation she said, "You mean nothing?"

I said, "Absolutely nothing."

"Then God help us," she cried.

"You've got it," I said. "That's it!"

This message is exactly what Paul has been telling us in these first five chapters of Romans. Everything is grace. Then he begins the sixth chapter with a question: "What shall we say then? Are we to continue in sin so that grace may increase" (NASB)? He answers this rhetorical question adamantly in verse 2: "May it never be! How shall we who died to sin still live in it" (NASB)? Then comes an amazing affirmation and challenging call in verses 3–4:

> Or do you not know that all of us who have been baptized into Christ Jesus have been baptized into His death? Therefore we have been buried with Him through baptism into death, so that as Christ was raised from the dead through the glory of the Father, so we too might walk in newness of life. (NASB)

The key ending of this passage is "walk in newness of life." Because of what Christ has done for us, we are new persons. Paul says, in effect, "Walk as though you are new persons; walk in newness of life."

In Ephesians we find a summary statement for the Christian life: "There is one body and one Spirit, just as also you were called in one hope of your calling; one Lord, one faith, one baptism, one God and Father of all who is over all and through all and in all" (Eph. 4:4–6 NASB). This is a comprehensive assertion which Paul sets in the context of our Christian calling: "Therefore I, the prisoner of the Lord, implore you to walk in a manner worthy of the calling with which you have been called" (4:1 NASB). The key ending of this passage is "walk . . . worthy of the calling." Other translations convey the admonition in terms of living or leading a life worthy of the vocation.

This charge is not only for the Ephesians and Romans of the early Church. This charge is for us today. Thus, it demands our reflection and full attention in this essay.

## Being a Christian—Already But Not Yet

Mark this fact: there is nothing static about the Christian life. Hear this shocking word from John Wesley's *Journal*:

> My friends affirm I am mad, because I said I was not a Christian a year ago. I affirm, I am not a Christian now. . . . For a Christian is one who has . . . love, peace, joy. But these I have not. I have not any love of God. . . . though I have given, and do give, all my goods to feed the poor, I am not a Christian. Though I have endured hardship, though I have in all things denied myself and taken up my cross, I am not a Christian. My works are nothing, my sufferings are nothing; I have not the fruits of the Spirit of Christ. Though I have constantly used all the means of grace for twenty years, I am not a Christian.[2]

Wesley recorded that assessment on January 4, 1739—about eight months after Aldersgate! It had been at Aldersgate where, after years of struggle, John Wesley came to a point of justification by grace through faith and assurance of salvation. His testimony from May 24, 1738, had been, "I felt my heart strangely warmed. I felt I did trust in Christ, Christ alone for salvation: And an assurance was given me, that he had

*Paul says, in effect, "Walk as though you are new persons; walk in newness of life."*

taken away my sins, even mine, and saved me from the law of sin and death."

Any reader of Wesley's *Journal* must wonder, *What's going on here?* Eight months after his Aldersgate experience Wesley is emphatic: "*I am not a Christian.*" The big issue we must not miss is the point of his turmoil. He's wrestling with himself and agonizing as Paul did in Romans: "I know that nothing good lives in me, that is, in my sinful nature. For I have the desire to do what is good, but I cannot carry it out" (Rom. 7:18 NIV).

> *There is nothing static about the Christian life.*

Can Wesley be a Christian and not be a Christian at the same time? There is no doubt about the fact: Wesley was a Christian; yet he was not a Christian. This statement is not double-talk.

In his *Journal*, Wesley was pouring out his soul. He was anguishing over his relationship with God. Of course, he already had been laid hold of by Christ. Wesley's situation may have been similar to Paul's sentiment:

> *Not that I have already obtained all this, or have already been made perfect, but I press on to take hold of that for which Christ Jesus took hold of me. Brothers, I do not consider myself yet to have taken hold of it. But one thing I do: Forgetting what is behind and straining toward what is ahead, I press on toward the goal to win the prize for which God has called me heavenward in Christ Jesus. (Phil. 3:12–14 NIV)*

While Christ had laid hold of Wesley, Wesley would make no claim to have attained the fullness of what he knew was his by Christ's gift and promise. This Pauline attitude must be our stance as well. This is the Christian stance: to be aware of what is yet lacking in our process of being perfected in Christ, and to press on to "take hold of that for which Christ Jesus took hold of me." So, Paul would continue to admonish us to "walk in newness of life" (Rom. 6:4 NASB). There is truly nothing static about the Christian life.

## At Home in Daylight

Earlier we noted Paul's call in Ephesians to "walk as children of Light" (5:8 NASB). In this passage Paul is calling the Ephesians to renounce the dark pagan ways in which they have lived. I like how the New English Bible (1970) and the updated Revised English Bible (1989) translate Paul's contrasting admonishment: "Live like men who are at home in daylight" (NEB) and "Prove yourselves at home in the light" (REB). We as Christians are to be "at home in daylight."

In the following paragraphs let us play with this grabbing image. I will come at it from a negative and positive angle. First, the negative perspective: To put it simply, to be at home in the daylight means that we cannot do those things in the night that would embarrass us in the light.

I remember a number of counseling sessions with a young man whose marriage was on the rocks. There were a lot of problems, and all of them were complicated by an adulterous affair on his part. He was one of the most sensitive persons I've ever known— sensitive to a fault, really. Not the least cause for the mess he was in was his inability to say "no" to anyone and to make decisions for fear of hurting others. Believe it or not, he also was keenly sensitive about his relationship with God. We never had a session where he failed to talk about God.

Forgiveness also was a big issue with him. So, he was a guilt-ridden person. When he had confessed his adultery to me, he wanted to know how he would ever overcome his guilt. I think he expected a theological answer or theologically deep conversation. He was taken aback, then, when all I said was, "Stop doing what is causing your guilt." Those few words were all I really had to say. Of course, we continued the conversation, but the essence of my admonition to him was to stop his destructive behavior, to stop sinning. The way to get rid of guilt is to stop doing what is making you feel guilty.

I saw a bumper sticker sometime ago that said, "Worry is like a rocking chair . . . it's something to do, but it won't get you anywhere." We could change that to read, "Feeling guilty is like a rocking chair . . . it's something to do, but it won't get you anywhere." Guilt is a gift from God that makes us realize something is wrong and needs changed in our lives. We can't be at home in the light if what we do does not have Jesus' approval.

Now the positive perspective: Paul put it, "Find out what pleases the Lord" (Eph. 5:10 NIV). The Christian life is a matter of doing what is pleasing to God. Paul did not say, "Be quiet; be passive; wait on the Lord as children of light and the light will grow in you." No, he didn't say anything like that. Rather, he said, "*Walk as children of Light.*"

> *We cannot do those things in the night that would embarrass us in the light.*

In so saying, Paul binds together two things: the divine working of the Holy Spirit within us and the human effort at redemption, retention, and application of that divine work. In the same vein Paul says, "continue to work out your salvation with fear and trembling, for it is God who works in you to will and to act according to his good purpose" (Phil. 2:12–13 NIV). God's light is within us; the living Christ indwells us. But, we have a responsibility too. We must choose to walk as children of the light. So, the Christian life is not only a matter of not doing what is displeasing, but of doing what is pleasing to the Lord.

Wesley talked about all of this as a prudential means of grace: doing no harm and doing all the good one possibly can. The truth of the matter is that we *live* our way into Christlikeness. We must *walk* in the light and live as people who are at home in the daylight.

## Advent throughout the Year

I have heard of preachers telling their congregations to celebrate Easter or Christmas throughout the year. But I don't recall ever hearing a preacher telling people to celebrate Advent throughout the year. Advent as a time of great anticipation really is an ideal season to keep in mind throughout the year and throughout our lives. As Christians, as resident aliens, as the body of Christ, we seek to walk with great anticipation between the "already" reality of God's kingdom and the "but-not-yet" reality of God's reign on earth as we know it. Thus, Advent encapsulates a spiritual attitude which can help us walk the Christian walk. Churches that skip Advent and celebrate only Christmas end up failing to truly appreciate Christmas for all it is. The gift of Christ at Christmas cannot be appreciated if we have not hoped for His arrival in a spiritual way.

Anglican Church tradition has preserved the ancient practice of praying several times through the day: at morning, midday, evening, and night. During the season of Advent the prayers and verses emphasize the theme of light. Here is a prayer or verse for each period of the day.

Morning:
Blessed are you, Sovereign God of all,
to you be glory and praise for ever!
In your tender compassion,
the dawn from on high is breaking upon us
to dispel the lingering shadows of night.
As we look for your coming among us this day,
open our eyes to behold your presence
and strengthen our hands to do your will,
that the world may rejoice and give you praise,
Father, Son and Holy Spirit:
Blessed be God for ever!

Midday:
O God of truth, O God of might,
you order time and change aright,
and send the early morning ray
and light the glow of perfect day.
Extinguish every sinful fire
and banish all our ill desire;
and, while you keep the body whole,
shed forth your peace upon the soul.
O Father, that we ask be done
through Jesus Christ, your only Son,
who, with the Spirit, reigns above,
three Persons in one God of love. Amen.


Evening:
Blessed are you, Sovereign God, creator of light and darkness!
As evening falls, you renew your promise
to reveal among us the light of your presence.
May your word be a lantern to our feet
and a light upon our path,
that we may behold your glory coming among us.
Strengthen us in our stumbling weakness
and free our tongues to sing your praise,
Father, Son and Holy Spirit:
Blessed be God for ever!


Night:
Look down, O God,
from your heavenly throne
and illuminate the darkness of this night
with your celestial brightness,
and from the children of light
banish the deeds of darkness;
through Jesus Christ our Saviour. Amen.[3]

## That Must Be Jesus

I close with a word that deserves to be extrapolated into its own essay: Paul admonishes in Colossians, "As you have received Christ Jesus the Lord, so walk in Him" (2:6 NASB). The amazing fact is that we do not simply follow Christ—which could lead to following Christ in our own power. Rather, we allow Christ to live in us. Thus, our *walk* becomes a "Christ walk."

There is mystery in this phenomenon. Picture the mystery the way little three-year-old Ryan did: He and his five-year-old sister, Lisa, were playing on the floor following a family dinner while the adults tried to hold a conversation. Lisa proceeded to unwrap a new toy, a physician's kit. She then convinced Ryan to be her first patient. She took the stethoscope and placed it on her brother's chest, listening intently for his heartbeat. Suddenly, she announced, "I hear somebody walking around in there."

To which Ryan matter-of-factly responded, "Why, that must be Jesus."

We all should respond the way that three-year-old boy did. Christ is the indwelling presence who enables us to walk the Christ walk. Our calling is clear: "As you have received Christ Jesus the Lord, so walk in Him" (Col. 2:6 NASB).

NOTES
1. William Barclay, *The Gospel of John: Vol. 2* (New York: Hyperion Books, 1993).
2. John Wesley, *The Journal of John Wesley* (Chicago: Moody Press, 1974), 137.
3. The European Province of the Society of Saint Francis, *Celebrating Common Prayer* (London: Mowbray, 1992), 63–85.

# CAREER AND CALLING

*Steve G. W. Moore*

MANY OF US PROBABLY WOULD BE BETTER FISHERMEN IF WE
DID NOT SPEND SO MUCH TIME WATCHING AND WAITING FOR
THE WORLD TO BECOME PERFECT.

—NORMAN F. MACLEAN
*A RIVER RUNS THROUGH IT*

Career . . . calling—two words that appear to be different ways of saying the same thing. Though they sometimes are used interchangeably, they are actually very different terms with distinct meanings that should not be confused. *Career* is the term most often used to describe what enables one to make a living. By career we usually mean a job or some form of employment, whether in industry, a profession, or some other field. It is hoped one's career carries with it remuneration and benefits that support one's livelihood and desired lifestyle. Careers that are financially rewarding often require diligent preparation through ongoing training or education—not to mention lots of hard work.

*Calling* is about making a life. A synonym of calling is vocation—*calling* is simply an Anglo-Saxon term, and *vocation* is its Latinate equivalent. When Christians talk about calling, the focus commonly tends to be on how a person uses all that God has given them. Christians understand that God grants each individual a unique set of gifts, passions, competencies, personality traits, and life experiences.

With the first part of the Great Commandment in mind ("love the Lord your God with all your heart, all your soul, and all your strength," Deut. 6:5, NIV; cf. Matt. 22:37; Mark 12:30; Luke 10:27), the Church understands that God's blessings are not to be used for selfish gain but for God's glory.

With the second half of the Great Commandment in mind ("love your neighbor as yourself," Lev. 19:18, NIV; cf. Matt. 22:39; Mark 12:31; Luke 10:27), Christians know that they glorify God by utilizing His blessings in service to others.

Frederick Buechner captures this sense of service when he defines calling as "where your deep desire meets the world's great need."[1]

## Three Misconceptions

### *Misconception #1: It's All about Me!*

Religious and non-religious people alike will frequently talk of calling in terms of what brings them a sense of fulfillment or satisfaction. Here the focus is on self-gratification and takes on what is commonly labeled a hedonistic attitude. Even people of faith fall into this trap. Louie Giglio, founder of the Passion movement, chides Christians for taking their focus off of God:

> I am tired of Christians walking up to me and asking, "How can I find out God's will for my life?" The question is not, "What is God's will for my life?" The question is, "How does my life fit into God's will? How can my life advance the will of God right now here on earth?"[2]

We need to ask ourselves, what is God doing, where is Christ's kingdom being advanced, how is the Spirit moving, and how can I be a part of that?

### Misconception #2: Worldly vs. Holy

When some people employ the term "calling" or "vocation," they are talking specifically about a career as a member of the clergy or a call into holy orders. This understanding can lead to laity feeling as though their lives in "secular" jobs are worth less than the clergy's "sacred" jobs. In short, this understanding amounts to a modern dualism about calling. John Stott, one of the outstanding Christian leaders of our day, observed such dualism:

> We often are given the impression that if a young Christian man is really keen for Christ he will undoubtedly become a foreign missionary, that if he is not quite keen as that he will stay at home and become a pastor, that if he lacks the dedication to be a pastor, he will no doubt serve as a doctor or a teacher, while those who end up in social work or the media or (worst of all) in politics are not far removed from serious backsliding![3]

The Christian response to this misconception should be to dispel any sense of a so-called "sacred" versus "secular" dichotomy. Everything is sacred! Yahweh God created the universe and everything in it. God is the master of all things. Everything is under the sovereignty of God. Therefore, all occupations and callings must be submitted to Christ's will.

Yet, too often, Christians persist in a mentality of

*All occupations and callings must be submitted to Christ's will.*

seeing missionaries and pastors as being in so-called "full-time" Christian work, while the rest of the Church are considered part-time Christian workers at best. Brian Walsh and J. R. Middleton, in their provocative book *The Transforming Vision: Shaping a Christian World View*, write:

> Even when we reject this notion of full-time service and say that all Christians are full-time servants of the Lord, an uncon-scious dualism may still constrain us. We often mean that we are all called to evangelize, no matter what situation we find ourselves in. In this case submission to Christ may still be limited to a so-called spiritual activity that is unrelated to the actual work of a secular occupation.[4]

Again, everything is sacred. This fact means that every moment of our lives is breathed to bring glory to God. Whatever occupies our waking hours—from rearing children to teaching neurosurgery, from cleaning toilets to being president of the United States, from milking cows to playing jazz piano—ought to be done as service to Jesus and in the presence of God. Brother Lawrence's example advises well:

> For me the time of action does not differ from the time of prayer, and in the noise and clatter of my kitchen, while several persons are together calling for as many different things, I possess God in as great tranquility as when upon my knees at the Blessed Sacrament.

> . . . I turn the cake that is frying on the pan for the love of Him, and that done, if there is nothing else to call me, I prostrate myself in worship before Him, Who has given me grace to work; afterwards I rise happier than a king. It is enough for me to pick up but a straw from the ground for the love of God. . . . to do our common business purely for the love of God, to set His consecrating mark on all we lay hands to . . .

... the littleness of the work lessened not one whit the value of the offering, for God regards not the greatness of the work, but the love which prompts it.[5]

### *Misconception #3: It's All Been Decided*

Additionally, when certain Christians influenced by flawed theological thinking consider the topic of calling or God's will, they assume that God has preordained a singular occupation for each and every person. One of the hallmarks of this type of thinking is that God predestines or plans out every event and action before it happens. In this view of the world there is very little room for human free will or choice. This scheme of things also lends itself to people feeling as though God allows very little room for error in life. That is, if God has predestined the way things are supposed to be, then people had better be sure that they know exactly what God's will is for every facet of their lives so that they don't somehow take a mistaken turn and veer off of God's road atlas. By the way, this way of thinking also infests our view of mate selection: if God predestines life, then He also must have already chosen whom I am supposed to marry, which means that I had better find the one person in the world that God wants me to marry or I'll be in trouble. Such an understanding can lead to much stress and strain as a person mulls over every single detail of life, seeking to "discover" God's will for his or her life.

Lawson Stone, a biblical scholar, comments:

I fear too many students talk about vocation in a way that allows wrong theology to influence their thinking about vocation. They talk about finding God's will for their lives in a way that interprets God's will as some mysteriously hidden and secret roadmap that once found will reveal to them every turn they are supposed to take in life. Meanwhile—while being detoured by trying to ferret out this roadmap—students bypass God's will that is already in plain daylight. They neglect and ignore the Word of God that has already been revealed to them.

The will of God has already been revealed to us. It's in the Bible.[6]

Further clarification of this point comes from a thoughtful book, *Decision Making and the Will of God: A Biblical Alternative to the Traditional View*, by Garry Friesen and J. Robin Maxson. In their helpful and extensive work, the authors explain that rather than a hidden divine will regarding each person's calling and life decisions (what they label the "traditional view"), God has endowed us with wisdom to discern which ways of turning are consistent with the overarching call to be a Christian ("way of wisdom").[7]

Friesen and Maxson point out several faults of the traditional view including the following: One, in cases of equal options, "insistence upon only one 'correct' choice generates anxiety over 'missing the dot,' rather than gratitude for more than one fine opportunity." Two, "the traditional view tends to promote immature approaches to decision making" by denying the reality of equal options, downplaying reason, delaying decisiveness, encouraging the practice of "putting out a fleece," and by using justifications, such as, "God told me to do it" or "God led me this way." Three, the traditional view leads to subjective decision making by neglecting the fact that through the special revelation of the Bible "God's moral will has been completely revealed and the means of acquiring wisdom has been explained; the knowledge required for decision making is fully attainable."[8] Instead, the traditional view insists on conducting a wild snipe hunt for another source of objective knowledge of God's will.

In the very last chapter of J. R. R. Tolkien's *The Lord of the Rings*, Samwise is faced with a dilemma of how best to use a magical seed to restore the beauty of the shire. He wants to do what the Lady Galadriel would want him to do with it:

"What can I do with this?" said Sam.

"Throw it in the air on a breezy day and let it do its work!" said Pippin.

"On what?" said Sam.

"Choose one spot as a nursery, and see what happens to the plants there," said Merry.

"But I'm sure the Lady would not like me to keep it all for my own garden, now so many folks have suffered," said Sam.

"Use all the wits and knowledge you have of your own, Sam," said Frodo, "and then use the gift to help you work and better it."[9]

About a year later Sam encounters the Lady who greets him with these rewarding words:

"Well, Master Samwise," she said. "I hear and see that you have used my gift well. The Shire shall now be more than ever blessed and beloved." Sam bowed, but found nothing to say. He had forgotten how beautiful the Lady was.[10]

## Differences

"So why can't career and calling be the same thing?" you may ask.

"They're supposed to be the same thing," would be my short answer. The better answer takes longer. Calling is bigger than career. Calling is what shapes our true identity, what brings us meaning, and what guides our lives—including career pursuits. Without a sense of calling, career becomes empty and absurd. Calling without career remains an aloof abstraction with no concrete relationship to the world in which we live.

Lee Hardy of Calvin College writes,

Work and vocation are not the same thing. Work may be a part of my vocation, but it is not the whole of my vocation; work may be one thing that I am called to do, but it is not the only thing I am called to do. . . . My vocation has many facets. If I am gainfully employed, my employment will count as only one of those facets.

If we are asked what our vocation is, we are expected to say what we do for a living. It follows that finding one's "calling in life" is a matter of finding an occupation; that a person without a job is also without a vocation; and that the aspects of a person's life outside work do not have the dignity of being vocations—they are merely the insignificant details of personal life.[11]

With the close of the Cold War which had preoccupied nation states in the latter half of the twentieth century, the United States had great expectations for more peaceful times in the third millennium. Radical Muslim terrorists, however, brought those hopes crashing down. In the light of such deplorable *modus operendi*, Christians can't quite fathom why Islam is growing exponentially in some sectors of the world while Christianity is losing adherents.

*Calling is bigger than career. Calling is what shapes our true identity, what brings us meaning, and what guides our lives.*

Perhaps one not insignificant factor is that some of these radical Muslim terrorists are people attempting to live out their faith and sense of calling in every sphere of their lives, even to the point of death. Such misdirected radicals are repulsive to Christians. Yet, however grudgingly, we have to admit that people are drawn to leaders who not only proclaim a compelling vision of life but actually live it out.

As Christians, we must ask ourselves, *Do my words and life match?* Tom Sine notes in *Mustard Seed Versus McWorld*:

In the first century, being a Christ follower was not something you worked in around the edges of an already overcommitted life. Following Jesus was clearly a whole-life proposition that caused people in that first community to reorder their entire lives to put God's purposes first.[12]

Sadly, many Christians today seem to lack such an integrated faith that lends itself to living life holistically. If Christians can rediscover the art of articulating a sense of calling, then Christians may have a chance at living lives that reflect the integrity of a life that is compelling and honors God!

## Discernment

Regretfully, career is the main emphasis in society. For one thing, a career is more concrete and easier to manage than a calling. In fact, our society has become quite efficient and effective at career management. It's even a burgeoning industry with human resource specialists, headhunting firms, resume writing services, and career consultants filling the marketplace. Google returned 3,530,000 hits for "career center"! Most institutions of higher education and large towns have a career center where people can learn about drafting resumes, searching for jobs, and interviewing tips.

*As Christians, we must ask ourselves, Do my words and life match?*

And while these are essential and important skills for life, there's a much more crucial concern looming in the minds of most people that seldom gets discussed: *How do I discern my calling?*

Unfortunately, there is nothing neat or tidy about discerning one's calling. It requires hunger to know oneself, a desire to love God, and a willingness to serve. Os Guinness puts it this way: "A sense of calling should precede a choice of job and career, and the main way to discover calling is along the line of what we are each created and gifted to be."[13] In other words, instead of "You are what you do," a calling says, "*Do what you are!*" So ask yourself, *Do I know yet what I am?*

> *Instead of "You are what you do," a calling says, "Do what you are!"*

Those who have spent a significant portion of their lives in Christian circles are used to listening to people talk about "hearing a call" or someone saying, "God told me to _____ (you fill in the blank)." As confident and assured as that may sound, the reality for most of us is that discerning our calling is as much about learning to listen to our own hearts as it is trying to hear other voices.

While I firmly believe that God speaks to us today, I have found that for most people, it is a still, small voice—not a booming basso profundo accompanied by thunder and flashing lights. Discerning one's calling is as much an art as a science. It sees the world through the eyes of the heart. It requires risk, daring to live in places where we are not in full control. It eschews expectations of any twelve-step process or easy-to-follow formula. It leads us to a place of vulnerability and wonder and imagination—all places where those of us who live in quick-fix, instant-gratification America don't always like to go!

## Frodo and Neo

Going these places, taking those risks, and spending time in discernment is worth it. It is *so* worth it! In fact, once you've had a taste of life lived with calling you can't go back. It's like Frodo and Samwise in their adventure in *The Lord of the Rings*. At the beginning of the epic they know they must leave their comfortably humble shire and face unknown dangers in order to fulfill their calling. At the end of the tale they realize their lives and the shire will never be the same.

It's also like Neo in *The Matrix*:

MORPHEUS: Do you believe in fate, Neo?

NEO: No.

MORPHEUS: Why not?

NEO: Because I don't like the idea that I'm not in control of my life.

MORPHEUS: . . . The Matrix is everywhere. It is all around us, even now in this very room. You can see it when you look out your window or when you turn on your television. You can feel it when you go to work, when you go to church, when you pay your taxes. It is the world that has been pulled over your eyes to blind you from the truth.

NEO: What truth?

MORPHEUS: That you are a slave, Neo. Like everyone else you were born into bondage, born into a prison that you cannot smell or taste or touch. . . . This is your last chance. After this there is no turning back. You take the blue pill, the story ends, you wake up in your bed and believe whatever you want to believe. You take the red pill, you stay in Wonderland, and I show you how deep the rabbit hole goes. Remember, all I'm offering is the truth, nothing more. Follow me. . . .

NEO: What does that mean?

CYPHER: It means buckle your seat belt, Dorothy, because Kansas is going bye-bye.[14]

After swallowing the red pill, Neo's eyes are opened to the way things really are. He realizes that he's been existing in a terrible dream world. His calling becomes clear: he must lead others out of the dream world and into real life, even if that means giving up the comfort of the lie.

Once you awaken the desire to be and do what God is calling you to be and do, the thought of a "career" seems pretty boring. A career can never be enough—at least, not enough for those of us who want to wake up out of our comfortable dream worlds and embrace the real reality of the kingdom of Christ.

"You are a chosen people," declares Peter, "a royal priesthood, a holy nation, a people belonging to God, that you may declare the praises of him who called you out of darkness into his wonderful light" (1 Peter 2:9 NIV). This is our corporate calling as Christians. God calls us out of darkness, and we in turn call others out of the same darkness. Our individual callings must find their niche within the overarching purposes God has for all of humanity to know Him.

## Five Buoys

The story is told about a ship seeking safe harbor on a stormy night. When the navigator radioed the harbormaster on the shore, she gave them these simple instructions: "Line up the five buoy lights in the harbor until they appear as one. Keep these lights in order and you will have a straight course into the harbor." I would suggest to you that discovering your calling is much the same. Let me suggest five principles that, when in line together, can help you set a course to your calling.

### 1. The One and Only You

First, and perhaps most obvious, is knowing and under-standing your gifts and talents. College is a great time to sharpen and clarify these. When I was young, I used to dream of playing in the NBA. But by the time I got to college, I was happy to be playing on a great intramural team! It had become fairly clear to me that I wasn't going to get "discovered" and that my talents didn't lend themselves to being an NBA player. I could scratch professional athlete off my to-be list.

But in college, I also had an opportunity to work with the youth at a nearby church and I discovered that I loved it. Close friends began to tell me I seemed to have a gift for getting people involved and encouraging people to consider Jesus as a friend instead of seeing God as the guy out to stop all the fun and make life miserable! I took note of these friends' insights into my gifts and talents. I also began to realize the importance of matching my gifts with my calling.

Have you ever asked people who know you well what they think your talents and gifts are? It may be kind of scary to do, but they can help provide important pieces of the puzzle—a key clue to your calling.

### 2. All That Jazz

A second principle helping you discover your calling is simply to ask, *What is it that really jazzes (excites) me? What motivates me? What is it that energizes me?*

I watched Rick each semester as he dutifully completed his architecture classes. He could do it and he could get As and Bs, but he wasn't very excited about it. When I finally asked him if he'd ever considered switching majors to something he might get excited about, he immediately remarked, "I would if I just knew what that was!" He was paralyzed by the unknown. One maxim of Maxie Dunnam, chancellor of Asbury Theological Seminary, is "Most of us prefer the hell of a predictable situation rather than risk the joy of an unpredictable one."

Escaping the hell of a predictable situation takes courage and strength. Rick found his courage. And together, he and I found the strength as we strategized on some steps to help him discover his passions. He started pursuing his emerging interests. One of those pursuits was going on a Habitat for Humanity work trip to Central America. While on that trip, a light went on—Rick came back motivated to combine his analytical and creative building skills with providing affordable housing for the poor. The course of his calling began to unfold!

Not everyone has that inner drive to propel themselves along the often difficult road out of the hell of predictability, but many do. Sometimes it needs to be encouraged, sometimes let loose, sometimes directed. Sometimes we gradually feel it welling up inside us as we begin to get closer to things that jazz us. At all times, we need the Holy Spirit and the willingness to listen and ask ourselves, *Does this energize me or drain me?*

The psalmist prays of God, "May he give you the desire of your heart and make all your plans succeed" (Ps. 20:4 NIV). Discovering what motivates you and what is your heart's desire gives you another clue to calling.

### 3. *The Real Real World*

One of the surprising trends in television programming since entering the twenty-first century has been the surging popularity of "reality TV." MTV network pioneered the emerging genre with its series *The Real World*. Though what viewers saw was often the result of heavy editing, manipulation, and clever scriptwriting, *The Real World* gained popularity because the casts seemed like real people who had real-life experiences like viewers might have or wished they had.

Experiences matter, both good and bad. Human tendency is to want to get through the bad ones as quickly as possible and hang on to the good ones as long as possible. There is one more possibility: learn from all experiences. One of the great promises of the Bible is that God desires to take everything that happens to us and weave it into good in the tapestry of our lives: "We know that God causes everything to work together for the good of those who love God and are called according to his purpose for them" (Rom. 8:28 NLT).

My wife, Thanne, and some friends often went waterskiing in college. On one trip, an accident occurred and one of their friends received a horrible head injury. During the course of the friend's long recovery, Thanne watched as therapists helped the young man put his life back together. It inspired her to look into speech therapy, which eventually became her calling and career. Today, she has helped thousands of head-trauma and stroke victims recover or develop the means to communicate again. I've watched in wonder and amazement as she tenderly yet determinedly works with people. An unexpected life experience became the bridge to an unexpected call.

A young woman came to graduate school unsure about her calling but hungry to do God's will. In 1997, she heard about a course that included a trip to India, so she signed up. While traveling and seeing the various missions and ministries at work in that amazing subcontinent, she couldn't help but notice that everywhere they went, there were children on the streets. Upon graduation, she decided to go to India and open a home for unwanted children. If you visited India today, you would find that she has become "Mom" to more than sixty children who are growing and thriving under her loving care.

Experience is another piece of the puzzle, another buoy in the harbor guiding the way to go. What are the experiences you've had or need to have that may help unfold your future?

### 4. Who's That Knocking?

"It seemed like a huge open door . . ."

"The door just seemed to slam shut in my face . . ."

Open doors. Closed doors. Listening to people talk about discerning their callings and God's will, one usually hears a lot about the way in which opportunities and circumstances play an important part in discerning one's calling.

The tough thing is, not every open door is a door you should walk through. At certain points in life many of us will have more opportunities than we can use, requiring that we make some tough choices between equally good options.

Closed doors, obviously, prevent us from entering new opportunities. On the other hand, not every closed door should be interpreted as a "Do Not Enter" sign. Sometimes closed doors are simply challenges through which we must persevere as we continue down the path we're on. Sometimes opportunities are temporarily disguised as obstacles! Sometimes closed doors will detour us toward a better direction and an open door we otherwise would have never noticed or considered.

Nonetheless, it is a fair and reasonable assumption of faith that God will use circumstances to nudge us in the right direction. We must be careful to not let circumstances be the only factor guiding our understanding and discussions.

The apostle Paul provides a great example of someone who sensed an open door and entered (2 Cor. 2:12–14), who experienced a closed door and went another direction (Rom. 15:22–29), and who used bad circumstances to accomplish good things (Phil. 1:12–14). One of the characteristics of Paul's life was that he surrounded himself with people who became his partners and fellow-travelers in seeking and following God's calling. That leads us to the fifth principle to be used in concert with the four already mentioned: the principle of community.

> *Not every open door is a door you should walk through.*

### 5. We Are Family!

Let me make a rather bold statement: You will not discover God's calling or God's will by yourself. It will involve and include other people.

Have you seen the television series *Joan of Arcadia*? It is the story of a young woman who learns to listen to God in everyday life. God sometimes comes to her as a telephone lineman, as an old woman in a bookstore, a little girl on a playground, or in some other unexpected form. God tells her, "I try and speak to people all the time, but that doesn't mean anyone listens."

Though the show isn't meant to teach sound theology, the principle is still very true: God often speaks to us through other people. Only more often than not, it is not through strangers, it is through people who know us well: a teacher, a coach, a youth pastor, a family

*We need people in our lives who will encourage us to dream big.*

member, or a friend. We need people in our lives who will encourage us to dream big, challenge our thinking, evaluate our planning, and believe in our abilities.

Gerald Sittser, in his book *The Will of God as a Way of Life*, quotes Elisabeth Elliott's encouragement to find people to be a part of our lives. She shares that she has been blessed:

> in having several friends of my own age who have helped me often. But I have been especially blessed through the advice of men and women much older than I. They see things I don't see. They've been over roads I've never traveled. They have perspective I couldn't possible have.[15]

One friend who does that in my life is Don. He has been working hard to discover and follow God in a deeper way. As a retired businessman, he is realizing that the attitude we are called to cultivate in order to hear God's leading is "an attitude not marked by self-reliance, self-sufficiency, or control, but rather by a willingness to be led to places not so comfortable and not so predictable." He goes on to say, "it just may be the answer to the spirit-infused longing that so many desire, and struggle to define. And as counter-cultural, counter-intuitive, and uncomfortable as it may appear to be, it may be the key to the transformation of the Church—and you and me!"[16]

**There you have them:**

- Know your gifts and talents.
- Understand what motivates and inspires you.
- Be attentive to experiences, both good and bad.
- Consider open doors and closed doors.
- Surround yourself with, and get input from, people who know you and who can help you understand the other four principles.

As we seek to line up these five buoys in the harbor, we do well to remember one final word. Sittser quotes the writer and teacher Frederick Buechner who said that the most important voice in recognizing our calling is "the voice that we might think we should listen to least, and that is the voice of our own gladness."[17]

## NOTES

1. Frederick Buechner, *Wishful Thinking: A Seeker's ABC* (San Francisco: Harper Collins, 1993), 19.

2. Louie Giglio, unpublished sermon notes (Asbury Theological Seminary, April 2003).

3. John Stott, *The Essential John Stott: A Double Volume for a New Millennium* (Downers Grove, Ill.: InterVarsity Press, 1999) 221.

4. Brian Walsh and J. R. Middleton, *The Transforming Vision: Shaping a Christian World View* (Downers Grove, Ill.: InterVarsity Press 1984), 64.

5. Brother Lawrence, *The Practice of the Presence of God: Brother Lawrence* (New Kensington, Pa.: Whitaler House, 1982), 18, 83.

6. Lawson Stone, unpublished lecture notes (N.p., 2004).

7. Garry Friesen and J. Robin Maxson, *Decision Making and the Will of God: A Biblical Alternative to the Traditional View* (Sisters, Ore.: Multnomah, 1980), 82.

8. Ibid., 90.

9. J. R. R. Tolkien, *The Lord of the Rings* (New York: Random House, 1981), 387.

10. Ibid., 389.

11. Lee Hardy, *Fabric of This World* (Grand Rapids, Mich.: Eerdmans, 1990), 19.

12. Tom Sine, *Mustard Seed Versus McWorld* (Grand Rapids, Mich.: Baker, 1999), 33.

13. Os Guinness, *The Call* (Nashville, Tenn.: W Publishing Group, 1998), 45.

14. "Down the Rabbit Hole," *The Matrix* DVD, directed by Andy and Larry Wachowski (Burbank, Calif.: Warner Bros. Home Video, 1999).

15. Gerald Sittser, *The Will of God as a Way of Life* (Grand Rapids, Mich.: Zondervan, 2000), 151.

16. Don Mowat, unpublished remarks (Asbury Theological Seminary, January 2004).

17. Sittser, *The Will of God as a Way of Life*, 170.

**SUGGESTED READING**

*The Call* by Os Guinness (Portland, Ore.: W Publishing Group, 1998).

*Decision Making and the Will of God: A Biblical Alternative to the Traditional View* by Garry Friesen and J. Robin Maxson (Sisters, Ore.: Multnomah, 1980).

*Fabric of Faithfulness* by Steve Garber (Downers Grove, Ill.: InterVarsity Press, 1996).

*An Incomplete Guide to the Rest of Your Life* by Stan Gaede (Downers Grove, Ill.: InterVarsity Press, 2002).

*Let Your Life Speak: Listening for the Voice of Vocation* by Parker Palmer (San Francisco: Jossey-Bass, 2000).

*Living the Life You Were Meant to Live* by Tom Paterson (Nashville, Tenn.: Thomas Nelson, 1998).

*Mustard Seed Versus McWorld* by Tom Sine (Grand Rapids, Mich.: Baker, 1999).

*The Transforming Vision: Shaping a Christian World View* by Brian Walsh and J. Richard Middleton (Downers Grove, Ill.: InterVarsity Press, 1984).

*What Color Is Your Parachute* by Richard Bolles (Berkeley, Calif.: Ten Speed Press, annually updated).

*Why You Can't Be Anything You Want to Be* by Arthur F. Miller Jr. (Grand Rapids, Mich.: Zondervan, 1999).

*The Will of God as a Way of Life* by Gerald Sittser (Grand Rapids, Mich.: Zondervan, 2000).

*Your Work Matters to God* by Doug Sherman and Bill Hendricks (Colorado Springs: NavPress, 1987).

# THE CONTOURS OF A CALL

*Ellsworth Kalas*

THE ESSENCE OF REAL INTELLIGENCE IS THE SKILL IN EXTRACTING
MEANING FROM EVERYDAY EXPERIENCE.

—UNKNOWN

It seems that the call of God isn't what it used to be. I first realized as much during a conversation with a friend of some years, a man whose ministry had begun with a small holiness denomination and had gradually evolved into a very effective series of congregations in the Episcopal Church. Now in his retirement, he was reminiscing on the changes that had occurred in his lifetime.

"In our day," he said, "we were called to *preach*. There was nothing general about the call. It was very specific: Preach." My memory told me he was right. In my youth I never thought of describing myself as having a call to the ministry, and certainly never to a broadly ambiguous term, "I have a call." I was called to *preach*. The literature of two generations ago, whether in books or periodicals, used the same language; the call from God was a call to preach. The only exception was "a call to the mission field." This was seen as specific in its locale—that is, outside the United States—but more generic within that locale, probably because everyone knew that a missionary did many things, with preaching only one item on the list.

Then a change came. I suspect that the doctrine of a call developed as have most doctrines: after practical and pragmatic factors have been at work, theologians define the specifics of the doctrine. The phenomenon may have begun with denominational administrative roles which pastors filled, sometimes temporarily and sometimes permanently; in the Methodist tradition, for example, district superintendents and bishops evolved. I suspect that there was just a hint of doctrinal down-putting in the humorous way pastors often responded to colleagues who were becoming superintendents—"Oh, so you're leaving the ministry." But then some began to understand or to acknowledge that administration could be a calling from God; after all, the very word *administer* was built on the word *minister*. Perhaps, then, an administrator was not just a pastor who had become an executive; rather, administration was itself a calling. In some instances, it might even be a lifetime calling.

With this understanding came a new perception of a wide variety of ancillary roles. Consider the pastor who had left the preaching ministry to become the administrator of a denominational hospital, or the fund-raiser for a hospital or a church college; the preacher who became the editor of a religious publication; and in some cases the pastor who became a YMCA executive or the head of a branch of the Goodwill Industries. Where once colleagues had whispered of such persons, "They just couldn't cut it in the ministry," now they began to recognize that such offices could as assuredly be a call from God as the call to preach.

Another factor was also at work. A few pastors are still alive who remember the day when a pastor might serve a congregation of a thousand or fifteen hundred members with no more employed staff than a church secretary. Such a pastor preached, taught, counseled (though the term itself might not have been used), visited in hospitals and homes, and generally represented the church in community life. Such a pastor could not have imagined a church where he (and in those days the masculine pronoun covered the calling) would head up a staff with perhaps a business administrator, a youth pastor, a director of Christian education, a program minister, a pastoral visitor, and an associate pastor.

This development within local church administration reflected what was happening in the world of business, government, education, and yes, sports. Where once a university football team, or even a professional football team, had a head coach and two or three assistants, now there were assistants not only for defense and offense but for each "skilled position." The Age of Specialization had come. A popular joke from the era:

"I'll bet that National Cookie has a vice president for Fig Newtons."

"I can't imagine it. Call them and ask for him."

When the one who had raised the issue called National Cookie and asked to speak to the vice president for Fig Newtons, the operator answered:

"Do you want the vice president for Fig Newton manufacturing, the vice president for Fig Newton sales, or the vice president for Fig Newton development?"

Topical humor draws its laughs from exaggeration and absurdity. What is absurd in one generation, though, is a standard of excellence in another and old hat in the next.

I repeat: the Church followed this development in the contemporary culture. Not only was the day of the renaissance person gone from the field of knowledge, the generalist (or more colloquially, the jack-of-all-trades) was gone from medicine, from business, from sports, from government. The explosion of knowledge not only made ancient theories uncouth, it also compelled a whole new era of specialization. No one could be expected to know enough about any field to make all the decisions. There would never be another George Washington Carver in science, a Connie Mack in baseball, or a family doctor who prescribed aspirin, delivered babies, and performed major surgery.

So in the Church, a person no longer felt a call to preach but a call to ministry. That ministry might be education, pastoral care, counseling, business administration, youth work, missions education, visioning, or—yes!—preaching.

Consider the wonder. While all of this development might appear to be simply a replicating of the specializing that was happening in the secular world, it was in truth a perhaps awkward fulfilling of the pattern laid out for the early Church. As the apostle Paul wrote to the church at Corinth, "The gifts [Christ] gave were that some would be apostles, some prophets, some evangelists, some pastors and teachers, to equip the saints for the work of ministry, for building up the body of Christ, until all of us come to the unity of the faith and of the knowledge of the Son of God, to maturity, to the measure of the full stature of Christ" (Eph. 4:11–13 NRSV).

> *The work of Christ is too big, too complicated, too eternally challenging to be encompassed in one title or one calling.*

Paul's language may sound foreboding compared to ours, but the point is the same. The work of Christ is too big, too complicated, too eternally challenging to be encompassed in one title or one calling. Perhaps in the process of redefining God's call, we have drawn closer to the New Testament standard for the Church. Our language may be a bit pedestrian compared to Paul's, and it sometimes may seem closer to the language of contemporary patterns of leadership and administration than to the language of theology, but the basic point remains. We have come to recognize that the call of God is larger than simply the call to preach.

As much as I cherish my lifelong sense of call that for me was singular in its focus (though multiple in the way it has been lived out), the present sense of call is closer to the New Testament than was the perception of my generation.

This new pattern is not only more biblical, it is also wonderfully exciting. I think of a friend who grew up in an executive's home and who apparently inherited his father's executive skills. Along the way he felt a call. Since he was part of a generation that still perceived God's call as primarily, perhaps even exclusively, a call to the pastoral ministry with a focus on preaching, he prepared himself for such a ministry. He served in the parish ministry for several years and did so reasonably well, but always I think with a sense of frustration. In most of his work he was exercising talents that were his secondary or tertiary skills, and only rarely was he using the gifts with which God had most notably empowered him. Then he found his way into the field of administration, specifically, the administering of denominational homes for the aging. His career there has been extraordinary. The good he has done for the kingdom of God fills me with awe. He has found his calling.

I could repeat this story with myriad variations. We have felt for a long time that persons might be called to serve God in the fields of music and of teaching, and yet only a few denominations actually have a track of ordination for persons who intend from the beginning to serve God in these ways. We have let them work in the Church but have been slow to certify their divine calling by a title of any sort. The United Methodist Church now has an order, a diaconate, that recognizes their work as a calling, a calling as valid as the call to preach.

As John Robinson, pastor to the Pilgrims, said, "There is yet more light to break forth from God's Holy Word."[1] Jerome, in the fourth century, got it right: "*Sacerdotium laici, id est baptisma*"; that is, "Baptism is the ordination of the laity."2 To be baptized is to have accepted a call. Protestants are proud that Martin Luther restored to the Church the doctrine of the priesthood of believers. Unfortunately, we have honored it more in the lapse than in performance. We think it's a noble idea, but most of us would have to confess that we rarely see this idea in action. Someone has said that the doctrine of the priesthood of all believers was not to destroy the priesthood and leave a Church of laypeople but to destroy the laity and leave a Church of priests. We are, indeed, all of us to become a called people, a people who recognize that to be a believer is to be called to ministry.

What has happened, perhaps even in the best of churches, is to convince Christians that they are called to sing in the choir, usher and greet, serve on committees, work in the kitchen or in special repair projects, and give leadership in the church school or the various social and service projects of the Church. I don't mean to minimize any of this; after nearly forty years as a parish pastor, I have profound regard for those faithful churchmen and churchwomen who give their time and abilities so generously to the Church in particular and to the community in general. But is there more to the call than this?

> *To be a believer*
>
> *is to be called*
>
> *to ministry.*

That is, could it be that every Christian is, in truth, called of God; that every honorable kind of occupation can be a holy calling? Was Noah called? Without a doubt! To what, then, was Noah called? It appears that he was called to be a shipbuilder. Was Abraham called? I venture that no Old Testament personality was more surely and definitively called of God. To what calling? To preach? If so, there is no evidence of it. He was called to be a father to many nations, via his unique fatherhood for Isaac. Was Moses called? He had a phenomenological experience to prove his call, a bush that burned and was not consumed. What was his call? Again, was it to preach? If so, he made a strong case against such an assignment when he argued with God about the limits of his oratorical skills. Instead, Moses demonstrated dramatically a call to be a liberator, a lawgiver, and a national leader who worked with a collection of raw material that demanded genius. He had the genius, because he was *called*.

The Church has had its moments and its exemplars. I think of William Wilberforce. On Sunday, October 28, 1787, young Wilberforce (only twenty-eight years old at the time) wrote in his journal, "God Almighty has set before me two great objects, the suppression of the Slave Trade and the Reformation of Manners."[3] In time, Wilberforce led England to make slavery illegal. It was a slow process, and much of the time a discouraging one. Slavery was so woven into the economic fabric of England and of much of the rest of the world—including those Africans who were complicit in the slave trade—that many felt industry and commerce could not exist without slavery. Nonetheless, Wilberforce prevailed, partly by his genius as a politician within the British Parliament and by his oratorical skills, but even more by the faith commitment which energized him, even when he was constantly vilified and at times physically assaulted.

Along the way, Wilberforce also succeeded in his second aim, "the Reformation of Manners," by which he meant making possible a whole new way of life and morals for subjected elements of the population. He succeeded with vigor and imagination, at one time leading or actively sharing in sixty-nine different initiatives for reform.

On first glance, Wilberforce was an unlikely man to spearhead such altruism. He was born to affluence and comfort. At twenty-one, he was elected to Parliament and, young as he was, quickly began to assume positions of recognition and leadership. Because of his upbringing and inherent advantages, he seemed positioned to become a voice for privilege. By doing so, he could have anticipated a political career that would know few bounds. Instead, he became a voice for the least powerful elements of society, people who could do nothing to further his career and who would instead prevent its predictable success. What happened?

I am impressed that even completely secular sources explain Wilberforce's story by pointing to what they describe as his conversion to "Evangelical Christianity."[4] In 1785, while in his fourth year in Parliament, he experienced a sound and deep conversion. Even though he was so thoroughly involved in politics, he felt with his conversion that he should enter the ministry.

It was John Newton, the Anglican clergyman who wrote "Amazing Grace," who persuaded Wilberforce otherwise. Newton wrote, "It's hoped and believed that the Lord has raised you up for the good of the nation."[5] Wilberforce thought and prayed and cast his vote with Newton, his spiritual mentor. In 1788, he wrote in his journal, "My walk is a public one. My business is in the world; and I must mix in the assemblies of men, or quit the post which Providence seems to have assigned me."[6] This outlook reflects the language of someone who knows he or she is *called*. No wonder, then, that an encyclopedia says of Wilberforce that his antislavery ideas were a product, not of his politics, but of his religious beliefs.[7]

Let me be clear. I don't see Wilberforce simply as a politician or a statesman with deep Christian convictions, much as I honor such a stance and much as I wish there were a hundred such in every state. I see him as a person who felt he was called of God to do what he was doing. In my judgment, he was as much called to his post as Billy Graham, E. Stanley Jones, and Pope John Paul II were to theirs. I suspect that when Wilberforce was converted, some earnest, pious folks pondered how wonderful it would be if such a talented person were to receive a call to the ministry. I submit that he was, but that his ministry was in the halls of Parliament.

Dag Hammarskjold would have understood. Hammarskjold was elected secretary-general of the United Nations in 1953 and was reelected in 1957. He was in that post in the most perilous of times, as numbers of African peoples began their unsteady journey from colony to nationhood. He lost his life in that struggle in an air crash while flying to what was then Northern Rhodesia to negotiate a cease-fire. In his journal, which was published after his death, Hammarskjold had once written, "In our era, the road to holiness necessarily passes through the world of action."[8] In a foreword to the journal, W. H. Auden wrote, "A reader of *Markings* may well be surprised by what it does *not* contain—that Dag Hammarskjold should not make a single direct reference to his career as an international civil servant, to the persons he met, or the historical events of his time in which he played an important role."[9]

We can understand this remarkable man only if we read another entry from his journal, a startling look into his soul. "If you fail," he wrote to himself, "it is God, thanks to your having betrayed Him, who will fail mankind. You fancy you can be responsible *to* God: can you carry the responsibility *for* God?"[10]

When Hammarskjold wrote that "the road to holiness necessarily passes through the world of action,"[11] I like to think that he was speaking specifically of his own relationship with God. I am satisfied that there are those who are called to a cloistered life, whether in the structured life of a monk or a nun or in the pattern of the often unknown Protestant saint whose basic ministry is prayer. But if by chance Hammarskjold intended to speak for all when he called for the "road to action," I will disagree with him only while confessing that his emphasis on action is no more at error than the theology that sees holiness expressed only in purely religious terms.

If Hammarskjold made much of the road of action, he sensed that the action was sometimes in a realm that is difficult for the secular mind to define. He turned to the language of the apostle Paul: "There are actions—justified only by faith—which can lift us into another sphere, where the battle is with 'Principalities, Dominions and Power.' Actions upon which—out of mercy—

41

*everything* is staked."[12] He saw the perils of power and success better than many of us in the professional clergy when he reminded himself, "It was when Lucifer first congratulated himself upon his angelic behavior that he became the tool of evil."[13]

In a sense, it isn't too difficult to imagine someone being called to the world of civic service, even when we define civic service with the tainted word, *politics*. After all, we have a biblical precedent. Moses was a political leader, as we have already noted, as were Samuel and David, and later Josiah and Hezekiah. Indeed, the strategic difference between the ten northern tribes of Israel who lost their identity in captivity and the southern tribes who survived to be the people of God is probably this: that the southern tribes now and then had a king who sought the ways of the Lord and who believed that the anointing that was upon him was more than a ritual, while the northern tribes never had a ruler that followed the commands of God.

> *Is it possible to be called to the world of business?*

Is it also possible for a person to be called to the world of business? Once again, I want to emphasize my definition. I am speaking now not of a businessman who works with Christian principles, even to the point of beginning his office day with prayer. I thoroughly admire such persons; I have been pastor to people of such deep and earnest faith. But in this paper I am going a step farther. Is it possible to be *called* to the world of business?

Herbert J. Taylor would say so. During World War I, young Taylor enlisted in the U.S. Naval Reserve, and as a lieutenant (junior grade), he was sent to the U.S. naval base in Brest, France. When the war ended, the navy gave him a short leave of absence to become regional director for the YMCA, to assist in care of service personnel as they passed through France en route home. Taylor saw the YMCA—which at the time was more clearly identified as a specifically Christian organization—as perhaps his calling to serve God. At the same time, he also was entertaining a job offer with Sinclair Oil Company.

After prayer, Taylor felt he should confer with George Perkins, a partner in the J. P. Morgan firm who had befriended him. When he laid out his options to Perkins, the executive answered, "You think I'm going to tell you to go with the YMCA, don't you? Well, that's not what I'm going to tell you. I suggest you go into business." The financier said that because of Taylor's "God-given business talent," he would succeed with Sinclair, so much so that he would someday have his own company where he could "influence the making of policies," and from that base, devote more and more of his life to Christian activities. Taylor was surprised by Perkins's answer.

"From the moment I left Mr. Perkins's office," Taylor wrote years later, "I knew the course of my life. It was one of the most confident and wonderful moments in my life." Taylor continued, "There isn't anyone on this planet who, if he will seek his *own* plan from God—sincerely, patiently, and with prayer, through Christ Jesus our Lord—won't have the facts revealed to him sooner or later, in one manner or another."

Taylor moved along so well that by the time he was thirty-seven, he was executive vice president of Jewel Tea. He left the security of that position to become president of Club Aluminum Products Company at a salary less than one-fifth of his previous position and with a company in such straits that "any three creditors could have gotten together and thrown the company into bankruptcy." He did so with a conviction that he could save the jobs of the company's 250 employees.

His job became an exercise in conscience and faith. When he received a tear sheet of some advertising, he found that his product was described as "the greatest cookware in the world." He instructed his advertising manager to eliminate all superlatives from their future advertising; no more "best" or "finest" or "greatest." He wrote out what he meant to be the guiding principles of his company, in twenty-four words:

1. Is it the truth?
2. Is it fair to all concerned?
3. Will it build goodwill and better friendships?
4. Will it be beneficial to all concerned?

He called it "The Four-Way Test." It has since become the worldwide motto of Rotary International, the world's oldest service club.[14]

Taylor's story from that point is in many ways a story of superlatives. As Club Aluminum gained solvency, he and Mrs. Taylor established a nonprofit foundation, to which they gave twenty-five percent of the company's stock. Through contributions from that stock and through almost unlimited investment of Herbert Taylor's time, a number of parachurch organizations were either started or dramatically increased in their influence, including Young Life, InterVarsity Christian Fellowship, and Child Evangelism Fellowship.

Taylor served a term as world president of Rotary International. In the last twenty years of Taylor's business career, he gave nearly all of his time and his extraordinary business genius to community and Christian organizations.

As far as he was concerned, the whole remarkable story began with the day he recognized his—if I may use the term—*call* to be a businessperson. When he left George Perkins's office, he knew the course of his life. He had sought counsel prayerfully and came out assured of his call.

I am writing with extraordinary idealism. I also suspect I am being willingly naïve. I think I would have been happy, when I was a pastor, if only a substantial proportion of my congregation had sought passionately to practice their Christianity in the way they taught school, ran their corporations, played football, managed their time, performed their surgeries, and operated their farms. But I believe there is a more excellent way. More than that, I submit that it is the biblical way (as one would expect a more excellent way to be), and that it is one grounded in sound doctrine. The realist in me insists that no matter how idealistic, it is a position worth preaching and teaching, because even if we don't achieve the ultimate, we will come closer to the penultimate because we have aimed for the ultimate.

One day, a young man raced to Moses to tell him that two otherwise unknown men, Eldad and Medad, were prophesying in the camp. Joshua, Moses' aide, rose to the challenge, urging Moses to stop them. "But Moses said to him, 'Are you jealous for my sake? Would that all the Lord's people were prophets, and that the Lord would put his spirit on them,'" (Num. 11:29 NRSV). As someone who has cherished his call

> *I believe there*
>
> *is a more*
>
> *excellent way.*

to the ministry since before his preteen years, I wish that all God's people knew themselves to be called. More than wishing, I think it should be so. Ideally, biblically, it should be so. Surely every human is as entitled to this grand sense of purpose as I am.

What would the Church look like if its members saw themselves as possessors of a *vocatio*? Consider, for instance, the decision many women have faced when they have felt compelled to choose—at least for a significant period of their career life—among serving as a full-time mother/homemaker, or being employed entirely outside the home, or seeking to combine the two roles. Many Christian women have contemplated the decision prayerfully, but perhaps few have done so theologically. Is it possible that one may be called to be a

*What would the Church look like if its members saw themselves as possessors of a vocatio?*

mother, and that this role would be chosen not by default or on the basis of economics or by a spouse's insistence or on the basis of peer influence, but on the assurance that this is one's *calling?* Conversely, is it possible that a woman may choose to be a surgeon, an office administrator, a professor, or a nurse because she believed this was God's call; so much so, in fact, that before she was "formed . . . in the womb" God had "consecrated" and "appointed" her (see Jer. 1:5).

So, too, with the newspaper reporter, the endocrinologist, the high school science teacher, the computer specialist, the taxi driver, and the manager of the grocery store. I am contending for the true nobility of any worthwhile work, and with such nobility the belief that one may be called of God to such a work. Ours is a wonderfully complex universe, where each part of nature contributes in its own way to the survival of the planet and its inhabitants. How much more, then, ought we humans—the most intentional of the planet's inhabitants—see our place as an assignment from God? The difference, of course, is this: that the other elements in our planet fill their role without any choice on their part, while you and I will fill our assignment only if we choose to be sensitive to the call of God.

An ancient Jewish tradition promises that if everyone were to keep the Sabbath just once, the perfect age would come. I wouldn't dare hope for a world where everyone confessed their work to be a divine calling; that would be evidence that the perfect age had, indeed, come. I only want to estimate what would happen if a fairly substantial percentage of professed Christians were to see their daily task as a calling. The holy fallout would be awesome. Those with such a perception would arise in the morning, not simply to make a living, but to fulfill a life. They would feel compelled to pursue their work with integrity. They would find an extraordinary new value in themselves, a value quite beyond the title on their door (if they have one) and the size of their remuneration.

I suspect that at this moment some reader is saying, "I know preachers who don't feel that way, and they claim to be called." I'm sure you're right. One of the tragedies of the ordained ministry is that we preachers can lose our sense of call. Mind you, we may still declare it to be true, but somewhere it has ceased to operate in our lives. It is not enough once to have heard God's call; that call needs to be heard again rather often, with new clarity and new appropriateness.

So I write to the spiritual descendants not simply of Isaiah and Jeremiah, but also the descendants of Noah the carpenter, Abraham the explorer and entrepreneur, Moses the political administrator, Deborah the judge, Hannah the mother, and Josiah the king. Beyond doubt, each was called.

*The purposes of God in our world are really too large to be trusted entirely to pastors, bishops, and seminary professors.*

The purposes of God in our world are really too large to be trusted entirely to pastors, bishops, and seminary professors. To limit God's call in such fashion is to suggest that most of life is profane. I am convinced that God wishes that as much as possible of our world should be made holy. I wish, to paraphrase Moses, that all the Lord's people would know that the work they are doing is one to which they have been called.

**NOTES**

1. Robert Merrill Bartlett, *The Pilgrim Way* (Philadelphia: Pilgrim Press, 1971), 221.
2. George E. Sweazey, *Effective Evangelism* (New York: Harper & Brothers, 1953), 89.
3. David Vaughan, *Statesman and Saint: The Principled Politics of William Wilberforce* (Nashville: Cumberland House, 2002), 58.
4. Ibid., 51.
5. Ibid., 125.
6. Ibid., 97.
7. *Encyclopedia Americana*, international edition, s.v. "Wilberforce."
8. Dag Hammarskjold, *Markings* (New York: Ballantine Books, 1964), 47.
9. Ibid., Foreword.
10. Ibid., 17.
11. Ibid., 47.
12. Ibid., 48.
13. Ibid., 51.
14. Herbert J. Taylor, *The Herbert J. Taylor Story* (Downers Grove, Ill.: InterVarsity Press, 1968), 51–53.

# WHAT KIND OF BOOKMASTER
# WILL YOU BE?

*Bill T. Arnold*

FOR THE GRACIOUS HAND OF HIS GOD WAS UPON HIM.

—EZRA 7:9B NRSV

The congregation was so proud. I had been their pastor for a while, and things had gone well. Now I was just putting the finishing touches on a doctoral degree in biblical studies. The congregation held a small reception to celebrate and honor what Susan and I had accomplished. But . . . there was our little four-year-old son, running around telling everyone, "Oh, he's not the kind of doctor who can help anyone—he's a book doctor." I knew what he meant, and so did everyone else. My son's assertion, though, raised an interesting question: *What kind of doctor would I be?*

I meet lots of people in biblical studies who are book doctors, but not the kind who can help anyone. As a professor at a seminary I wonder, *What kind of book doctors—bookmasters, in fact—will my students be after they matriculate and commence into leadership roles in the Church and society? Will they be bookmasters who can help people?*

Ezra was the kind of bookmaster who helped his people. Imagine yourself back in the days of Ezra. Much had happened in the corporate life of God's chosen people Israel. The long, hard exile was over. Eighty years beforehand, the seemingly all-powerful Persian king, Cyrus, had graciously released the Jews living in exile in southern Mesopotamia. A few of them returned, rebuilt the temple, and finished the job in 515 B.C. But things didn't turn out the way they had expected. The little Judean province was just that—an insignificant cog in the giant political machinery of Persia. There was no obvious or visible Messiah to lead them into political strength and freedom; the land still lay in ruins; the walls of Jerusalem remained in disrepair; and the people largely were unaware of the old Sinai traditions, the importance of the Lord's covenant, and the code of ethics provided by the law.

In chapter 7 of the scroll named after him, we encounter the great scribe Ezra, who leads another return to the beleaguered city of Jerusalem in 458 B.C. Ezra soars high in the traditions preserved for us in the Old Testament, as his long genealogy in verses 1–5 illustrates. In fact, Ezra appears here as a second Moses. Just as Moses was the lawgiver, so Ezra is a new lawgiver. He, more than any other servant of God, stamped the restoration community of Judea with its lasting character as "the people of the book."

Most scholars believe that Ezra is the editor who collected and organized the old Israelite traditions, turning them into a "bible"—that is, the Torah—for the community of God. Ezra also successfully taught, preached to, and convinced the community that the Torah was right and true; and that they honored God by submitting to Him and by living out the Torah in their everyday lives. Ezra is truly a wonderful model of what it means to be a minister of the gospel for any community in any age.

As always, when the Bible offers a character as an example for our lives, the emphasis is not on how brilliant Ezra was, although the text acknowledges that he "was a scribe skilled in the law of Moses that the LORD the God of Israel had given" (7:6 NRSV). Neither is this text primarily interested in how rhetorically gifted Ezra may have been, nor how elaborate his preparation was. This is not the message of the narrative.

This fact becomes clear through the recurrence of causation in the phrase, "for the hand of God was upon him" (vv. 6, 9). In the immediate context of verse 9, the phrase, "the gracious hand of his God was upon him," refers to protection during a difficult journey over a five-hundred-mile trip from Babylonia to Jerusalem—a journey often plagued by dangerous animals and bands of thieves and marauders. The emphasis is not on Ezra, but on God's hand.

But that's not all. If we look a little closer, we discover that the phrase, "the hand of his God was upon him," occurs six times in Ezra chapters 7 and 8, and two more times in Nehemiah, but nowhere else in Scripture. This is a central theme for Ezra 7 and 8. Two of those occurrences imply protection over the long and dangerous journey. God places His hand, which is characterized as "good" or "gracious," upon Ezra; and He protects Ezra along the way in which He had called him.

At other times in these chapters, the expression refers to provisions, such as God granting to Ezra through the Persian king whatever he needed (7:6). Another time Levites are needed to minister in the newly built temple, and God's gracious hand is upon Ezra, providing the Levites (8:18). Later, when Nehemiah needs safe passage to Jerusalem and timber to rebuild the city and city walls, the text says the Persian king grants all these things because the gracious hand of God is upon him (Neh. 2:8).

In two places, our expression refers more generally to encouragement or strength (Ezra 7:28; Neh. 2:18). At the conclusion of Ezra chapter 7, Ezra praises the Lord for putting it into the heart of the Persian king to glorify the house of the Lord in Jerusalem and to act faithfully with Ezra. Therefore Ezra exclaims, "I took courage, for the hand of the LORD my God was upon me" (v. 28 NRSV).

This clause is central to our text. God doesn't call you to a task without also providing for you and empowering you to accomplish it. If God has called you and God is in it, you are—by definition—commissioned to accomplish it.

You and I need the good hand of God upon us. I know: My wife and I were married three months before I began seminary. Our idealistic bubble burst that fall when we moved into a roach-infested, dilapidated, old apartment, and had to hold down two jobs to pay for it. It wasn't easy—just as there were many hard days for Ezra.

> *God doesn't call you to a task without also providing for you and empowering you to accomplish it.*

This text does not say God removed all obstacles and made the calling to which Ezra was called easy to accomplish. Ezra testified to the protecting and encouraging presence of God while performing the task of ministry. Likewise, there were moments when my wife and I didn't think we'd ever survive seminary.

Nevertheless, with God's hand, we graduated and took our first appointment at Calvary United Methodist. Now we had really turned a corner. We graduated from our old, roach-infested apartment to an old, roach-infested parsonage, living on ten thousand dollars per year. But we never went hungry.

This phrase, "for the gracious hand of his God was upon him," characterizes the ministry of Ezra. The text refers to Ezra as "a scribe skilled in the law of Moses that the LORD the God of Israel had given" (v. 6 NRSV). Ezra preserved, exegeted, and applied that ancient Mosaic law of Yahweh for His new restoration community, for the new Israel. Just as you and I hear much of Matthew 28 as the Great Commission for the Church (and rightly so), I lift this passage to you as the Great Commission for Church leaders—for all bookmasters—the message of our text confronts us with an important question, "What kind of bookmasters will we be?"

There's more to this parallel with the Great Commission. Just as followers of Jesus make disciples by going, baptizing, and teaching, we understand from the first gospel what makes for effective disciple-making revealed in those powerful words, "and remember, I am with you always, to the end of the age" (Matt. 28:19–20 NRSV). We must be the ones who go, baptize, and teach. But we understand that the mission is not about us, and its success is not dependent upon us. Likewise, I invite you to consider this passage from Ezra as a paradigm for your effective leadership in the Church. It's not about your skills, your gifts, or talents. It's all about the good and gracious hand of our God upon you. Without that, your skills are impressive, but that's all they are. They're not effective ministry.

This fact brings us next to a critically important question. You say you understand that God's hand on your life involves vocation, preparation, provision, and strength. You want to be like Ezra; you want God's hand on your life to direct and empower you for effective ministry. But, most people in North America are prone to ask, "How do I get that? How can I achieve that level of accomplishment? How can I ensure success?" These very questions reveal our inability to appreciate the nature of Ezra's ministry.

Ezra 7:10 gives us the clear reason why God's hand was on Ezra. The causal relationship between verses 9 and 10 is clearly marked in the text, with the important little word *kî*, which—pun intended—provides the key that unlocks the significance of this text. "Ezra had set his heart to study the law of the Lord, and to do it, and to teach the statutes and ordinances in Israel." The presence of God's hand was really only a by-product of something else going on in Ezra!

One must not read this as the secret to building a great church and somehow turn it into a formula for producing great pastors. People born and raised in the entrepreneurial spirit of the United States of America all too quickly could take from this a recipe for successful church-building. But this text is about the character of Ezra and about those commitments in his life that built character.

Ezra was devoted to something larger than himself. This portrait of Ezra is a model demonstrating that we must be willing to embrace the fact that the work of the kingdom is not about us and it's not about building a big ministry. It's about giving ourselves to something outside of us, about throwing ourselves into a grand idea and purpose that is not of our own design or execution. Ezra set his heart on something.

What does this mean that he set his heart on something? We use the same little idiom when we say, "No use to argue with him, he's got his heart set on it." We mean that someone is stubborn; their mind can't be changed. Our expression is the negative version of the more positive biblical one. The heart represents the whole of one's being, the seat of the will. Ezra's fixated heart implies discipline, determination, initiative, and persistence.

This is not a gift of God's grace; this is no natural endowment that any two or three people may have but others simply can't have. This is an active decision that sets one's course in life. It's a commitment that overrides and overrules lesser commitments, determining how one invests one's life for God's kingdom.

The verb for Ezra "had set his heart" ("had prepared his heart," KJV/NKJV; "had devoted himself," NIV; or "had dedicated himself," NJPS) is the causative of the terms *establish* or *be secure*. It is to fix securely! Ezra was uncompromising; he was devoted. Note the three actions to which he devoted himself. Ezra was determined (1) to study the law of the Lord, and (2) to do it, and (3) to teach the statutes and ordinances in Israel (v. 10).

The term *study* is really to *seek* or *inquire* of the law of Yahweh. Thus, this verb indicates an active determination to learn the word of God. This denotation is, after all, the fundamental meaning of *disciples* as learners or pupils, and of *rabbis* as teachers. As the Great Rabbi Himself asserted, our task is to come to Him and learn of Him (Matt. 11:28–29).

A call to ministry is also a call to prepare for ministry, and a call to prepare for ministry is a call to study. All the great figures of Church history who have been used mightily by God were first prepared not only in their heart's devotion but in their willingness to love God with their minds. Whether I illustrate this point with Augustine, Calvin, Luther, or Wesley, I could affirm that these were individuals of not only great intellect but also rigorous training and preparation.

Wesley, for example, was an extremely well-read scholar. Yet he referred to himself on more than one occasion as "a man of one book." The most significant occurrence of this description in his writings is in the preface to his *Sermons*. In a passage full of autobiographical echoes, he portrays himself as a seeker after truth:

> I am a spirit come from God, and returning to God: just hovering over the great gulf; till, a few moments hence, I am no more seen; I drop into an unchangeable eternity! I want to know one thing—the way to heaven; how to land safe on that happy shore. God Himself has condescended to teach the way; for this very end He came from heaven. He hath written it down in a book. O give me that book! At any price, give me the book of God! I have it: here is knowledge enough for me. Let me be homo unius libri.[1]

Whatever it is we're about, we ought to be about devoting ourselves to the study of the Torah of the Lord. Now, please understand, I'm not referring to biblical studies as a discipline, nor even to biblical studies plus theology, philosophy, and Church history. The seminary where I teach has set its curriculum around the Torah of the Lord, the truth of God, as it plays out in all the disciplines of a theological seminary (e.g., Christian leadership and discipleship, counseling and pastoral care, evangelism and mission, homiletics and worship, ethics, and spiritual formation).

Asbury Theological Seminary, as an institution, is committed to the study of the truth of God as it relates to the world around us and as we're called to proclaim it to that broken world. For that reason, I've always found it appropriate and meaningful that, at Asbury, the chapel and library are side by side near the front and center of campus. The chapel is where the campus community worships corporately as a body. The library, which I take as a symbol for every classroom on the campus, is where students worship God individually—that's where we work hardest and best at loving God with our minds.

Dare I add, that's the primary objective of a theological seminary—being devoted to the study of the truth of God. The better we study that truth in the library, the more acceptable to God will be our worship in chapels and the more effective will be our ministry of service to the lost, the poor, and the downtrodden in the world around us.

The genius of Wesley was not his brilliance nor his fervor in evangelism but rather the combination of the Aldersgate heart with the Oxford mind. Don't ever lose sight of acquiring an Oxford-like determination to love God with your mind. Ezra had set his heart to *study* the law of the Lord.

Secondly, Ezra had set his heart to *do* the law of the Lord. Interestingly, this is the very common Old Testament word for *do* or *make*. In contexts of covenant keeping and obedience to the law of the Lord, it means "to perform, to carry out (a command)." At the most critical moment of the Sinai covenant, the people of Israel exclaimed, "All that the LORD has spoken, we will *do*" (Exod. 19:8, 24:7; cf. Deut. 5:27 NRSV).

Old Testament scholar of Israelite religion Helmer Ringgren says of this verb in the Old Testament, "to 'do' the ordinances, the commandments, the statutes, the Torah is to fulfill them, to translate them into action."[2] Ezra was determined to translate the Torah into action. That's the kind of bookmaster who helps people.

The Torah of the Lord, it turns out, is not some abstraction God wants us to memorize. The truth of God is not simply about routinely going through the motions and getting all the words right, nor some rote formula or ritual of speech through which we appease God and protect ourselves. In fact, I think we can draw from this text the idea that the genuine study of the law of the Lord is what drives Ezra to the commitment that he must *do* something. When you read the Bible rightly, you realize you must take action.

The more we learn of God and God's truth, the more we become aware of the call of obedience and integrity to act upon that learning—to move from *hearing* the word to *doing* the word (James 1:22, 25). We take action out of the love of God we develop from studying the law of God, not merely out of obligation. The more we learn of God, the more we love God, and the more we act on His behalf.

Each November, many professors from universities and seminaries around the world attend the annual conference of the American Academy of Religion and the Society of Biblical Literature. Every year at this conference I'm reminded of exactly how vast is the wasteland of much contemporary biblical scholarship. It is amazing to me how people who have devoted their lives to the study of Scripture can so often produce such arid and useless results. True biblical scholarship, no matter how meticulous the method involved, should never result in killing the fundamental message of Scripture.

*If you fail to study and do the word of God, you fail to prepare yourself for effective ministry.*

Now, it would be too easy for me to criticize those hundreds of biblical scholars who live in the biblical text but never apply it to their lives. Perhaps it would be more appropriate for me to ask my readers, "What kind of bookmaster are you becoming? Will you be like Ezra? Or are you jumping through academic hoops to satisfy the requirements of a degree program? Are you jumping through the hoops of denominational ordination requirements so you can get a church, where you will jump through hoops of the monthly and annual cycles of ministry?"

If you fail to study and do the word of God, you fail to prepare yourself for effective ministry—or, let me say, you already are failing in ministry and are setting yourself up for mediocrity in the future. Christians in postindustrial nations have a wonderful opportunity that many Christians around the world only dream of having: the opportunity to study theology, to become a bookmaster. If you have this opportunity, I charge you, in the strength of the word of God in this text: make up your mind to study the Torah of God and to translate it into action!

> *Make up your mind to to study the Torah of God and to translate it into action!*

I alluded earlier to the letter of James, "be doers of the word, and not merely hearers who deceive themselves." That passage continues by describing those who are hearers of the word as people:

> . . . *who look at themselves in a mirror; for they look at themselves and, on going away, immediately forget what they were like. But those who look into the perfect law, the law of liberty, and persevere, being not hearers who forget but doers who act— they will be blessed in their doing. (James 1:23–25 NRSV)*

Finally, Ezra had set his heart to *teach* the statutes and ordinances in Israel. Ezra made up his mind to teach the specifics of Torah-keeping to his people. This resultative *piel*, teach, implies that Ezra made it possible for his people, Israel, to learn what he had learned, to study the word of God and to translate it into action. Ezra was determined to learn, to act, and to reproduce himself in others.

If you're familiar with the books of Ezra and Nehemiah, you know that they seem to record what many assume is a chronological problem. We don't hear from Ezra again after this for over a decade. Ezra is said to have restored the people spiritually while Nehemiah did so physically, rebuilding the walls of Jerusalem. But when Nehemiah entered Jerusalem thirteen years after Ezra, he found many of the same immoral behaviors that Ezra attempted to correct. It was not until 444 B.C. that Ezra read the Torah to the people of God at Jerusalem's Water Gate, and the nation moved into a time of reform and renewal (Neh. 8).

So, which is it? Was Ezra successful or not? Did he build a great ministry of teaching and reform or didn't he? Is it possible that the silent decade missing from the record is because Ezra's ministry was not really successful? Or, as I would contend, is it possible that it took Ezra a decade to prepare for that one effective week at the Water Gate, where he read the Torah each day for the people?

The text of Nehemiah chapter 8 tells us that when Ezra read the law of God, the people didn't always understand it. Ready for this contingency, Ezra had a group of Levites there who had been trained for that moment. They "helped the people to understand the law . . . they read from the book, from the law of God, with interpretation. They gave the sense, so that the people understood the reading" (Neh. 8:7–8 NRSV). Is it possible that Ezra worked in quiet resolve for years, training Levites and teaching the Torah, waiting for one week like this, when he, by God's grace, could reach a nation?

Christians shouldn't be surprised by this possibility because, after all, half of the Great Commission (after *going*) is *teaching*. Half of making disciples of all nations is establishing new believers in the Word—enabling them to learn and do what we have learned and what we have done. After Pentecost, the first Christians "devoted themselves to the apostles' teaching and fellowship, to the breaking of bread and the prayers" (Acts 2:42 NRSV). I believe Ezra's silent decade in the books of Ezra and Nehemiah is intended to give us another model, another example of the faithful believer, quietly teaching, discipling in obscurity until that moment when his long, hard work burst forth in effective, nation-reforming ministry.

I grew up in the Church; I cut my teeth on the back of a Methodist pew and watched the Church from the inside out. Sadly, I've met a lot of cynical pastors in my day—a lot of jaded, sometimes bitter, burned-out pastors. In every case, each one started out as a young, enthusiastic seminary student who just wanted to get out of school and get started with ministry. The portrait in this text of Ezra is a good antidote for that ailment for those who would hear it. The good and gracious hand of God was upon Ezra because that which Ezra taught his people, he first lived; and what he lived, he learned from Scripture.

> *That which Ezra taught his people, he first lived; and what he lived, he learned from Scripture.*

If you make such a commitment—a commitment to study the truth of God, live it out in your lifestyle, and teach it diligently among your people—you stand in a very great heritage. We skimmed over Ezra's genealogy in Ezra chapter 7 verses 1–5, because we always skim over the genealogies—right? In the restoration community, though, genealogies were central. They were important to assure the people that they were indeed the people of God, that they belonged in Judah, and that they were within God's will. Furthermore, the genealogies were needed because the circumstances around them said just the opposite: they were insignificant and unlikely as people of God.

This little genealogy in verses 1–5 does not verify Ezra's right to serve, nor does it establish his authority, nor validate his message. His authority is rooted in the law he studied. These verses are there to remind Ezra and to remind readers of the tremendous heritage in which he stands. He is a son of the high priest, Aaron himself! He is surrounded by a great cloud of witnesses (cf. Heb. 12:1), upon whom the good hand of God has rested.

One of my treasured possessions, which I received from the Kentucky Annual Conference of the United Methodist Church the year I was ordained, is a list of names. It goes from my name to Bishop Frank Robertson, to Francis Asbury and Thomas Coke, to John Wesley, and all the way back to the apostle Peter. Now, I'm not High Church enough to believe that such a line validates me. Rather, it simply reminds me of my heritage. I stand on the shoulders of countless faithful servants. Some were famous, but many were not. God had His hand on them as He has His hand on me.

As a member of the body of Christ, you are part of a tremendous and holy heritage which is part of the Church universal. All of this is itself securely resting on the shoulders of Ezra and Aaron. With this reminder, I charge you: Allow the good and gracious hand of our God to rest firmly upon your shoulders. Commit yourself, make up your mind, set your heart on the study of the Word of God, and don't let anything prevent you from living it and teaching it in Israel.

NOTES

1. Albert Outler and Richard Heitzenreter, eds., *John Wesley's Sermon: An Anthology* (Nashville: Abingdon Press, 1991), 9.

2. Helmer Ringgren and G. J. Botterweck, eds. *Theological Dictionary of the Old Testament*, trans. J. T. Willis, G. W. Bramiley, and D. E. Green. 14 vols. (Grand Rapids, Mich.: Eerdmans, 1974), 11:394.

# Doubt, Dilemma, and Disenchantment: The Unforeseen and Underappreciated Detours of the Called and the Faithful

*Chris Kiesling*

The great end of life is not knowledge but purpose.
—Unknown

My calling is primarily to be a teacher. Every fall semester at the campus where I work we salute and welcome a new class of entering seminarians to campus. Optimism and freshness run high in the early chapel worship gatherings as we once again begin to compose a community for formation and learning.

Typically, one of the welcome week chapels is committed to an open forum in which students are offered the opportunity to give witness to the call of God on their lives and the myriad ways that He has worked to bring them to this place at this time in their lives. The testimonies never cease to amaze—the provision of housing and place for a spouse to work; the long trek from a foreign country to Wilmore, Kentucky; the unmitigated gift of a few years to study and grow; the entrustment and care of loved ones that were left behind; the unexpected gift of cash that was just enough. It always erupts into a litany of praise and gratitude.

And yet, despite being caught up in the offerings of thanksgiving and while sharing in the prayers for a deeper consecration toward my own calling at the academy, I am usually left wondering if there are other stories that do not get told in such a setting. Are there students who did not get a letter indicating a scholarship that would fully pay for their tuition? Are there spouses who were made miserable by the move, that did not want to interfere with God's call on their partner, but who felt little of the same compulsion to uproot from family, friends, and security? Are there those for whom the circumstances of their move worked against the confirmation of this being where they are called to be?

Consider the following scenarios that, although imaginative, emerge from actual experiences recounted to me in the struggle to discern and live out God's call.

*Karl was sitting in the airport lobby on a two-hour layover, reading a book he was not even sure why he had brought with him and that was proving to be even less engaging than the woman he had sat next to on the previous flight.*

*Now, finally alone with his thoughts, he tried to return again to the story until a single line from the book sent his mind drifting once again. It was the inward reflection of one of the characters in the book that he found himself strangely identifying with: ". . . life for him was going along meaninglessly well . . ."—the paradox in the phrase seemed to grab him, causing him to stop in his tracks and feel much the same way that he had felt earlier in the day when the Wal-Mart attendant accosted him for tripping the exit alarm and insisting that she needed to look inside his bag.*

*"Meaninglessly well . . ." it seemed to define a vague restlessness that had been stalking his life that, until now, he could not, or perhaps had chosen not, to name.*

*Indeed, "well" did seem to be a fairly apt descriptor of his life. Looking around at the people shuffling through the terminal, he reviewed in his mind the things he often looked to that formed his internal evaluation: a good wife who provided him a relatively happy marriage, a moderate degree of success in his work, kids who still respected him . . . and . . . well, he was sure he could name others. Still, the rest of the phrase nagged him . . . "meaninglessly well"? Was there something more that he was supposed to be about, something that had more purpose to it, more of an eternal value? Was God stirring this discontent in his heart, was it his own ego needing more satisfaction, or was it that large slice of airport pizza that was talking? He wondered what it would be like to change his vocation or even to take on a role at his church in one of the ministries that they offered. Did he really have the gifts or the patience with people to do something like that? And what about his past indiscretions—surely someone with his record wouldn't be someone that God could use . . . could He?*

*Anita felt trapped. She remembered the days in her campus fellowship where something latent was waking up inside of her. Worship, Bible study, and retreats with her spiritual friends had been nothing less than awesome. She*

*had developed a deep relationship with the living Lord and found such fulfillment in offering all that she was learning of herself and her heavenly Father to the small groups she was mentoring. Those were golden years in her memory. She was not displeased with the life that she was living now; it was, after all, much of what she had envisioned. It was just that the early years of raising kids and living her obligatory life for the sake of her family had left her with little of what she called her "Mary time"—sitting and soaking up the Word of God and sharing it in intimate spiritual friendships with others. (Heavy sigh.) There were still many years before the baby would be old enough to manage life on her own, and with added financial burdens, she was pretty certain that her husband would not be very supportive of her pursuing a costly education just to wind up in a low-paying ministry position on some church staff.*

*It seemed wrong to her to proverbially "bury the talent(s)" she believed God had given her, but how was she supposed to fulfill this calling if it increased anxiety to her family?*

*"God, where are you now and what the h—— are you doing to me?" Shelton was feeling desperate. Things were not going well in his ministry at the church and, as a result, he was feeling full of inadequacy, burnout, and incompetence all over again.*

*This was not at all what he thought God had in store for his life when he turned down the prospect of a good paying job in order to serve the Lord. Not only was he feeling somewhat betrayed, he also felt abandoned.*

*Theologically, he believed all the right stuff—God created the world and made humans in His image; He provided them with the good things of creation and offered Himself as an atoning sacrifice for sins when they went astray; He was a God who listened to prayers and took care of the sparrows of the field.*

*Still, the question that kept plaguing Shelton's mind was,* What has God done for me lately? *He felt that he had been led by the Spirit to take on this role in ministry, but where was the Spirit now, and when was the last time he had encountered God's presence? It felt like he was in an emotional desert wasteland and his parched spirit was drying up.*

*Antidepressants could stabilize his emotional turbulence, but this seemed deeper than a biological issue. He could soothe himself and quickly forget about it by visiting illicit images on his computer screen, but he knew that would only lead him to deeper despair and a diminishing of the little self-respect he had left. He was in the thralls of a spiritual battle and at stake was how he would spend the rest of his vocation.*

I chose as the title for this article "Doubt, Dilemma, and Disenchantment: The Unforeseen and Underappreciated Detours of the Called and the Faithful" because I wanted to convey that experiences like those of Karl, Anita, and Shelton are not at all uncommon. In fact, rather than being foreign to the pages of Scripture and, therefore, something to be avoided, it seems to me that the narratives of Scripture run toward, rather than away from, such encounters. They invite us to embrace such experiences as every bit a part of the journey implicit in calling. Reading the pages of Scripture, it becomes apparent that the call of God is rarely the shortest distance between two points. In fact, "the call" sends a person on a journey that often looks more like a bull ride than a peaceful ferryboat crossing. The experiences of doubt, dilemma, disenchantment, and the like, quite contrary to being something that suggest unfaithfulness, can become the very places where God does some of His most profound work.

## Doubt

The first point of crisis that most of us face when we begin to consider God's call on our lives is doubting that He could ever use someone like ourselves. We read the heroic stories of David killing Goliath; Esther risking her life to expose King Xerxes' right-hand man; or Shadrach, Meshach, and Abednego escaping the fiery furnace for their refusal to pay homage to an arrogant ruler, in much the same way that we read a biography of the rich and famous. It provides intrigue precisely because it seems so far removed from what will ever be the story line of our common lives. Because our lives and our abilities seem to pale in comparison, we discount ourselves from being the answer to the prayer we pray so perfunctorily—"Thy will be done in earth, as it is in heaven" (Matt. 6:10 KJV).

*The call of God is rarely the shortest distance between two points.*

Self-doubt has often been the first response of the called of God, and the excuses recorded in Scripture start sounding like "home cooking" when we get really honest with ourselves. Consider Moses as an example. God discloses His heart to Moses for an oppressed people and declares: "I am sending you to Pharaoh to bring my people the Israelites out of Egypt" (Exod. 3:7–11 NIV). In most translations Moses' response begins with what I recall my sixth grade teacher, Don Glidewell, calling a contrasting conjunctive, namely the phrase "But Moses." The contrasting conjunctive "but . . ." signifies the pairing together of a group of words, while at the same time signifying what makes the exception. In other words, Moses contends with God's call by claiming on the contrary, "who am I, that I should go to Pharaoh and bring the Israelites out of Egypt?"

Moses' objections are many: a fear of ineffectiveness reflected in his doubts that he won't be believed or listened to (Exod. 4:1–2); an accounting of his own frailties and lack of natural gifting to speak with influence (4:10–11); and a reasoned argument that the name under which he claims legitimacy will not be recognized (3:13).

Add to this that Moses must have been stewing in the wilderness for years in the shame of recognizing that it was his own flawed character that had forfeited what had undoubtedly been a life governed by the hand of providence. After all, his birth was a miraculous escape from infanticide. He was an Israelite raised by royalty and privileged with the best that Egypt had to offer. His own sister cunningly arranged to have his own mother serve as his nursemaid and be compensated for her services. He had been "saved," robed with title and status, and given a position of influence possibly essential for the survival of his people. Yet, in a rash act of anger that resulted in a murdered Egyptian, he fled into exile, regarding himself as an alienated man. Little wonder then that when God begins to impress upon Moses His compassion for the oppressed, Moses thinks Yahweh has the wrong man and at one point even pleads with God that He send someone else (4:10).

To note God's repeated response to Moses is to come to know something of the remarkable patience of the heart of God. Rather than shame Moses for his self-doubt and obstinate importunity, Yahweh makes it an occasion to reveal more of Himself to Moses. Whenever doubt is an honest doubt and not a smokescreen for some other agenda, God seems to honor such periods of suspended and partial faith by showing more of Himself to the person.[1] Notice the way Jesus responds to the doubts of Thomas by offering him His nail-scarred hands and feet (John 20:24–29).

When I was given the opportunity to apply for a professorship at Asbury Seminary, I knew that the role was far too big for me. Internally, I ran through all my defenses—*"I don't have the right 'stuff' to be a professor"; "I haven't suffered enough for the faith to be worthy of such a position"; "My graduate degree is in the wrong area"; "Others have had far more successful ministries than I have";* *"I don't even have good typing skills"*; and on and on. Still, friends in my covenant group urged me on.

> *Whenever doubt is an honest doubt and not a smokescreen for some other agenda, God seems to honor such periods of suspended and partial faith by showing more of Himself to the person.*

After the series of interviews that follow such a process, I approached my predecessor and mentor Donald Joy with the two questions I found myself raising: "Could I do this?" and "Am I really the person to do it?"

With wisdom abrupt enough to silence my protestations Don said, "The first question you can dismiss. We all have enough selfshame inside to keep us from saying yes to God's call. As to the second question . . . don't say no when the Church calls you." Then, in the profound way that Don so often taught his classes, he shared a story of one of his former students who didn't say no when recently asked by his bishop to come on the cabinet as one of the youngest district superintendents ever appointed in that conference.

Since then, I have thought often of the communal dynamic in the Scriptures that frequently surrounds one's sense of call. While in seminary, I was introduced to historical documents that offered distinctions between various types of calling. The theology undergirding these documents declared that: (1) all persons are called to a saving relationship with God through Jesus Christ and to renewal after the image of their creator; (2) all Christians are called to the ministry of servanthood whereby they witness in deeds and in words that heal and free; (3) some Christians evidence gifts and graces indicating a calling toward ordained ministry; and (4) every call entails both gift and responsibility.[2]

With doubt and shame in our lives we can easily discount ourselves from any aspect of that four-fold call, and so quite often we need others to validate the call being appropriated in our own lives. Whereas the call of God is personal and comes to us in many unique and various ways (as a process or in a crucial moment, growing naturally from our awareness of self and our giftedness or in a supernatural endowment, from our earliest experiences of God or late in our Christian walk), any call of God into ministry needs the confirmation and commissioning of discerning others.

I am wary of self-proclaimed prophets whose ordination by God has not been corporately discerned by the prophet submitting him or herself to the counsel of a recognized community of faith. In fact, rather than regarding it as just a series of "hoops to jump through," I have grown fond of our denomination's thorough and prolonged process of mentoring women and men in the process of discerning a special call to service, word, order, and/or sacrament, and I listen intently for the confirmation of others when trying to discern what God has called me to be and to do.

Let me return to Moses and to God's response to his self-doubt. The first thing God speaks into Moses' sense of self-doubt are the five words that anchor anyone's call—"*I will be with you*" (Exod. 3:12 NIV, emphasis added). When Moses dies, God says to Joshua, "As I was with Moses, so *I will be with you* . . . be strong and courageous" (Josh. 1:5–6 NIV). When Jesus looks through the corridors of time and places upon the eleven disciples the Great Commission, He says, "All authority . . . has been given to me . . . go and make disciples . . . And surely *I will be with you always*, to the very end of the age" (Matt. 28:18–20 NIV). Indeed, the antidote to our own inadequacies is the promise of the presence and the power of God.

Moses contends that he is not eloquent and is slow of speech and tongue. God prods Moses, "Who gave man his mouth? Who makes him deaf or dumb? . . . Is it not I, the Lord" (Exod. 4:11 NIV)? When Moses objects this time, it is no longer from a place of self-doubt but from a reluctance to trust that God is enough! God may acquiesce and provide Moses one to come alongside him as a helper, but He won't allow Moses to shirk His call. When God's word does speak decisively to the place of our doubts, and when His revelation provides adequately for our trust in His character, wallowing in self-pity ceases to be an option.

Myron Augsburger once recorded that there are three temptations that accompany Christian service—to whine, to shine, or to recline.[3] But God will have His way with us as He did with Moses. We may pray, "Oh God, make me a godly man or a godly woman!" only to come to the realization that it is through our weakness that His power is perfected (2 Cor. 12:9). If self-doubt is the first crisis most of us face in considering the call of God on our lives, a trust that becomes firmly established through long persistence is often the first reward.

## Dilemma

Mary, the mother of Jesus, comes to a place of great dilemma in following God's call at the most inconvenient time in her life (Luke 1:26–27). Most scholars reason that she is the equivalent of a young maiden, perhaps even in her teen years. She is in a committed relationship as a betrothed bride-to-be. If ever there was a legitimate time in her life to just focus on "me," it would seem that time was now for Mary.

In the midst of her forthcoming marital bliss, however, the angel Gabriel brings her a message that must have stirred her wildest imagination. She would conceive a child who would occupy the throne of David, a monarchy long deposed and belonging to a nation that existed only in dispersion. Further, what would it mean to be overshadowed by the Most High such that one would bear holy offspring (Luke 1:35)?

Somewhat like Moses, Mary's first reaction is puzzlement that Gabriel would visit someone like her. Astonishingly, it is not the fact that she has just been visited by God's archangel that startles her. Rather it's that the archangel of God addresses her as the "favored one." Mary's response to God's call is one of such full surrender and relinquishment that any reader unfamiliar with the story must have assumed that goodness would follow her "all the days of her life" for such devotion to a call from God and at such an early age—"May it be to me as you have said" (Luke 1:38 NIV).

However, life only gets more complicated and complex for Mary. The apparent illegitimate pregnancy no doubt gave the religious folk of her day something to talk about and it postponed the conjugal privileges of her relationship to Joseph (Matt. 1:25). Shortly thereafter is the trek to Bethlehem for Caesar's census and the weariness of there being no vacancy at any inn that then resulted in the barnyard birth. (One would think that if God were going to cause her miraculous pregnancy He might have called ahead to reserve a room in the hotel! Ha!)

The call of God on Mary only becomes more mysterious and costly. While Jesus is still an infant, Joseph has a dream that turns the family into refugees in Egypt (Matt. 2:13–15). There they learned that the birth of this child, and all the remarkable occurrences surrounding the heralding of His birth to the world, had now become the cause of Herod sweeping the country in a mass infanticide. Follow the story further and you discover that when Jesus is a teenager Mary and Joseph send out a missing child alert to all their friends and families when their adolescent son disappears for three days following Passover (Luke 2:39–52).

Years before, when Jesus was still a baby, a holy man had blessed Jesus and told Mary that by virtue of being the mother of this child "a sword will pierce your own soul too" (Luke 2:35 NIV). One can only wonder that with all that Mary had to "ponder in her heart," could she have ever fathomed that her son, who after all was "the perfect child," would suffer rejection, the worst of shame, and the fate of an unjust crucifixion? Dare we suggest that this was the call of God on Mary's life?

Not long ago, I replayed the tape of a sermon preached by Dr. Dennis Kinlaw. I listen to the message periodically in hope that I can spend the rest of my life living into its truth. Across every quarter of the twentieth century, Dr. Kinlaw's life has been intimately acquainted with evangelical thought and proclamation. On this tape, he recounted an article he had written whereby he sought for an expression that best captured the core value or obsession of evangelicalism across the century in which he had lived.

He determined that if there was a phrase that best captured what had been said to the twentieth century it would be an evangelistic word, announced in a variety of ways and toward a variety of needs. Indeed, whether it was the recognition of guilt that needed atonement for sin, the emptiness of the heart that yearned for purpose, or the offer of life beyond the grave, the predominant message Evangelicals had spoken to the world has been the message to "receive Christ." And to a great extent, the campaign has been a successful one.

However when the New Testament emphasizes the call of Christ on the lives of men and women, as Dennis Kinlaw notes, the fundamental invitation Jesus issues is not to "receive Me" but to "follow Me." "Whenever we talk about receiving," he continues, we focus on "what we get out of the relationship . . . Could it be that evangelicalism has contributed to part of the narcissism of our age?"[4]

His message suggests that when the fundamental understanding of our call changes, so do our questions that immediately follow. When the focus of the call is to receive Christ, the questions too easily become: *What can I get out of it?* But when the fundamental aspect of Christ's call on a person's life is to follow Him, we cannot escape asking the question: *Where am I going?*

And once we recognize that the place to which Jesus was traveling was to Jerusalem to carry His cross, we cannot help but realize that the cross is to define our calling as well. By this I mean that the cross moves us in our understanding of calling from a place of self-absorption to a place of personal involvement in feeling the brokenness in God's creation. Indeed, the cross defines the character of our calling by declaring decisively that our time, our talent, and our treasure is to be made an offering for the sake of the world's redemption.

Henry Blackaby and Claude King's powerful study, *Experiencing God*, names so well what I have referred to as the dilemma of the call. In spelling out the pattern of how we come to know and experience God, Blackaby and King recognize that God's invitation to work with Him is always accompanied by a crisis of belief. The crisis may entail a change of employment; it may set in conflict familial responsibilities and missional imperatives; it may mean contact with others that are undesirable and marginalized; it may require a relinquishment of financial security; it may engage you and others close to you in lifestyle change; it may involve taking on responsibilities that seem far too big; and/or it may involve an unpopular critique of conventional society. Yet beneath them all is God's design to have us come to share His burden. When we do, we find ourselves participating in an eternal drama that fulfills our wildest dreams.[5]

## Disenchantment

There is one more vocational hazard on the journey of call that I think gets little press but is equally common and equally intends our faith formation. I chose the term "disenchantment" because it implies the loss of something that at an earlier time attracted, roused, and moved one deeply.

In retailing religion for a consumeristic culture, it is not uncommon for churches and church leaders to put a lot of hype into religious experience. Eager to build vital congregations and to see people passionate for the things of God, there is a tendency to create liturgies and special events designed to maximize the affective encounter.

I support the legitimacy of making available crucial moments whereby grace is appropriated and leaps of faith are taken toward becoming conformed to the image of Christ and more fully aligned with God's call on a person's life. However, I think it is often true that what we win people *with* is also what we win them *to*.

Religious commitments grounded only in emotional experience create about as much staying power as romance has proven to hold people to their marital vows. Given two years or so, their sense of call or commitment, grounded in emotion, diminishes in its intensity. Accustomed or addicted to feeling "high," the subsequent letdown experiences may be characterized in a variety of ways—dryness, hitting bottom, ordinariness, wilderness wandering, depression, backsliding, spiritual attack, etc.

The causes of disenchantment may be multiple or there might not be any detectable reason at all. Typically, our sense of calling emerges from things about which we care profoundly and that have touched our lives at the deepest levels. Following a call often compels one to take on a role that is situated at what Parker Palmer calls "the dangerous intersection of personal and public life."[6]

The expectations of others, the tyranny of urgent demands, the disinterest or even antagonism on the part of those we serve can all collude against a secure sense of our calling. To reduce our vulnerability, suggests Palmer, we self-protect.[7] In doing so, many lose access to the passions that originally formed their call and find themselves "losing heart."

I have heard numerous stories where a person's sense of vocational call diminished upon their first exposure to ungodly behavior in the Church—"I can't believe people who call themselves Christians can act like that," they protest. Church politics are not immune from manipulation, dysfunction, or other more personal indiscretions.

I know of students whose sense of call was deflated by a lack of support from significant others in their lives (parents, spouse, mentor, etc.). Further, I remember a fellow campus minister sharing a burden he carried for ethnic minorities who struggled through college believing that education was the guaranteed prerequisite by which they could pursue their vocational calling, only to find upon graduation that the job market was not granting them immediate access.

I have received the support letters of those eager to answer the call to overseas missions but were discouraged, finding that raising financial support was more difficult than anticipated. I know of many who spent the early years of ministry trying to teach and preach from the overflow when their own souls were empty; many finally left ministry altogether.

*Disenchantment means "to free from illusion."*

I have counseled with many followers of Christ who confide that they know that their spiritual lives are not what they should be and have internalized a sense that "something must be wrong with me because I just don't feel close to God anymore."

What might God intend from such experiences?

There is an important second definition to the word "disenchantment" that I find helpful to remember when encountering such times. Disenchantment also means "to free from illusion." In this sense I think it names a process very similar to what many newlyweds discover in the first few years of marriage as the relational dynamics move them from a place of idealization to one of realization.[8]

Walter Wangerin reasons that marriage can pose such an intimidating commitment that we often need a strong persuasion to move toward it, a persuasion, he believes, is often induced by the idealization of the prospective partner. In common parlance, we give heed to this phenomena when we say, "Love is blind," or wonder, *"What is it that she sees in him?"*

In the same way we may idealize our call—overexaggerating our own current capabilities; playing out projected, internal dramas of the great movements we will lead for God; or imagining ourselves dying a martyr's death under the threat to renounce Christ. Such fantastical projections are formative, healthy, and I think even qualify as "sanctified imagination." Heaven knows we need more dreams of ourselves as moral exemplars, great revolutionaries, and those inhabiting a faith that moves mountains.

And yet, just as we discover that the real person we married has blemishes, peculiar habits, and hygiene that occasionally breaks down, so do we also find that there are aspects to "call" that are anything but glamorous, that people are not as responsive to the things of God as we imagined, and that our own gifts and graces require years of preparation and formation before they become acknowledged as the tool of God we fantasized them to be.

The transition from idealization to realization is neither superficial nor is it necessarily a quick passage. However, very significant formation and vocation often occur in the process. Consider a few biblical examples.

The initial call of God to Abram entails a promise that he would be given land, that he would be made into a great nation, and that through him all the families of the earth would be blessed. In this initial visit, it is primarily God who speaks and Abram appears as an obedient and compliant listener (Gen. 12).

As the narrative progresses, however, almost everything in Abram's life moves against the probability of this calling ever being fulfilled. First there is a severe famine in the land causing Abram to leave the very real estate God had just promised to give him. While finding food in Egypt, Abram himself threatens the promise, playing sexual jeopardy with his wife. Next comes a perpetual saga with his kinsman Lot that embroils Abram in land settlement, an intra-national war, and the witness of God's judgment being wrought upon Sodom and Gomorrah.

As the story unfolds further, we learn that Abram's wife is barren, compelling Abram and Sarai to hatch a plot in order to aid the Almighty with His part in fulfilling the covenantal call that promised them descendants. When God does finally open Sarah's womb and the child who will carry the covenant is born, God Himself moves against the promise and asks Abram to sacrifice the child.

What's so fascinating to note throughout the story is how Yahweh is at work fashioning Abram to be the father of many nations. Paul Borgman, in *The Story We Haven't Heard*, notes that there are six more visits God makes to Abram, at the heart of which stands God's word of assurance to Abram, "Do not be afraid" (Gen. 15:1 NIV). Borgman notes how Abram transforms through the process from "silent partner" to that of intercessor, learning to partner with God and increasingly, reflect the way God acts in the world.[9]

Or consider the call on the life of Joseph that first originates in consecutive dreams around the time when he was seventeen years of age (Gen. 37:1–8). Rather than winning him favor, it evokes rebuke from his father and jealousy and a conspiracy of hatred from his brothers against him. For thirteen years everything in Joseph's life spirals downward—thrown into a pit; sold to the Ishmaelites; betrayed by Potiphar's wife despite his integrity; and forgotten by those to whom he had employed his spiritual gifting. If ever there was cause for disenchantment it could be found in the pathos of Joseph's story, but instead we find cause for great promise.

Or consider the call to the Israelites to leave Egypt for the Promised Land. One day they stand on the banks of the Red Sea dancing in delight to have witnessed Yahweh's decisive victory over Egypt, and three days later they are in desperation, complaining that God's hand has been too short to feed or to provide (Exod. 15). The pattern of pledged commitment, followed by murmured discontent and unfaithfulness, continues until eventually God suspends their entrance into the Promised Land for forty years so that He can sift their hearts and bring them to a reliance on His words alone (Deut. 8:1–3).

Or notice how often in the New Testament crowds of disciples turn up when Jesus is performing miracles and dispensing the gifts of the kingdom coming, but when He issues the call to costly discipleship even the chosen apostles consider leaving (John 6:6–69). While physically present with the Twelve, Jesus systematically moves them through most every prevailing condition they may encounter in fulfilling their call to make disciples of every nation. Along the way Christ allows them to fail miserably at the task—slow in their understanding, lacking perception, misguided in their motives, weak in the disciplines that lead to spiritual power, fearful at some times and overly zealous at others—their idealization of Messianic hope causes them repeatedly to miss the reality of the mission of Christ. For them, the crucifixion must have been the greatest disillusionment of all.

I often take my students on a mental exercise by asking them the following questions, "If you were God—which, if you have not yet discovered it, you are not—but if you were God, how would bring your followers to know that there is a peace that passes understanding unless you were brought to a place where you had no understanding? How would you know that the kingdom of God belongs to those who are 'poor in spirit' unless God brought you to places where you are at the end of yourself and your self-reliance? How would you come to know Him as the 'Light of the world' or the 'Good Shepherd who pursues the lost sheep' unless you were allowed to encounter darkness and lostness? How would you learn that He is faithful and trustworthy unless He throws you into situations where you have to rely on something other than your natural giftedness or wits?"

When we follow this by recounting episodes in their lives when they experienced the greatest spiritual growth or when we ask them to interview those who possess a faith they would like to emulate and ask what has made their faith so enduring and rich, the awareness is almost always that it came through the valleys, in the hardest of times, and when they prayed because they had to.

So what is God doing in us through the experiences that I have called disenchantment and how does it relate to our sense of call? Implicit in almost all of the biblical narratives previously cited is that a long period of waiting often occurs between the initial call on a person's life and the point at which that call comes into fruition and/or the point at which the person emerges in full possession of the character and equipping God needed to create in them.

Waiting is often the posture of the people of God.[10] Waiting tests our reliance. Waiting often creates temptation and trial. Waiting creates the space in which we sort through a myriad of questions like: *Did I discern the call correctly? Can I really trust that God will open up a door to get me to a strategic point of ministry? What current experiences am I going through that are designed to help me become a person of endurance and godly reaction? Are there motives in my heart or wounds from my past that the Spirit may want to surface before I am cast into a position of responsibility where such distortions in my own soul would be inflicted on those I serve?* Waiting itself can be disenchanting, and if biblical history is any indication, the people of God have not fared well during such seasons.

What foundational truths might we come back to during the times in our lives when we cannot see clearly what God is up to or when we cannot answer with clarity how our present situation fits into His call on our lives? First, I think that those who live through a calling to its place of ultimate fulfillment rarely do so in our day and age as lone rangers. Those who sustain a calling through many years of service seem to do so because they have structures and people in their lives that keep the fire of their calling burning.[11] For many it is a mentor who was present when the call was first awakening in them to whom they can turn when their inspiration lulls; for others it's the vitality of a community that makes it plausible to live out one's calling despite the hindrances and weariness that often accompany it. For most, there is a need to nurture the convictional underpinnings of a call through spiritual readings, times of contemplative intimacy, meaningful worship experiences, and relationships that unpack the stuff of the soul.

*Regard it as a compliment when God removes external prompts and trusts you to follow His call.*

Secondly, we must appreciate that God is invested and at work in the process every bit as much as He is committed to the destination of our calling. It is often through the seasons of disenchantment that a new self is struggling to be born[12]—a self that has a deeper awareness of its frailties and strength, a self that is coming to entrust more of its future and place in the world into the gentle hands of our Good Shepherd.

I like the awareness it brings to observe that quite often when God wants to lead a person to greater faith, He leaves their prayers unanswered. Early in any relationship we look for demonstrations of how the other person feels about us,[13] and quite frequently when a person begins to pursue God's call on their life, He often seems to acquiesce to their need for reassurances of His presence and power in their lives. Like we raise kids to become less reliant on our constant attention, and we value when they begin to make their own judgments governed less by external influences and more by principles that have been internalized, so I believe we can regard God as honoring our growth and development when He moves us from overreliance on the demonstrative aspects of His provisions and more on what we know of the essence of His being and faithful acts throughout human history. Regard it as a compliment when God removes external prompts and trusts you to follow His call because a deep inner conviction is being born, not of emotion, but of solidified certainty.

I have collected prayers that have been meaningful to me throughout three decades of following God's call on my life. Every time I find myself at a critical juncture concerning that call, I take out John Wesley's Covenant Prayer. I find the words difficult to really take to heart, but I believe that they point to a relinquishment and surrender that honors God for being God and through which we come to entrust our lives to the Shepherd of our souls (1 Pet. 2:25).

> I am no longer my own, but Thine.
> Put me to what thou wilt, rank me with whom thou wilt.
> Put me doing, put me to suffering.
> Let me be employed by thee or laid aside for thee,
> Exalted for thee or brought low by thee.
> Let me be full, let me be empty.
> Let me have all things, let me have nothing.
> I freely and heartily yield all things to thy pleasure and disposal.
> And now, O glorious and blessed God,
> Father, Son, and Holy Spirit,
> Thou art mine and I am Thine. So be it.
> And the covenant which I have made on earth,
> Let it be ratified in heaven. Amen.[14]

NOTES

1. Os Guinness, *Doubt* (Downers Grove, Ill.: InterVarsity Press, 1976), 37.

2. *Book of Discipline of the United Methodist Church* (Nashville, Tenn.: United Methodist Publishing House, 1996), 96.

3. Myron Augsburger, *The Communicator's Commentary: Matthew*, Lloyd Ogilvie, ed. (Waco, Tex.: Word Books, 1982), 134.

4. Dennis Kinlaw, "A Hunger for Holiness," library series *A Vision for Holiness*, tape 1 (Wilmore, Ky.: Francis Asbury Society, 1991).

5. Henry Blackaby and Claude King, *Experiencing God: Knowing and Doing the Will of God* (Nashville, Tenn.: Lifeway Press, 1990), 184.

6. Parker Palmer, *The Courage to Teach* (San Francisco: Jossey-Bass, 1998), 39.

7. Ibid., 40.

8. Walter Wangerin Jr., *As for Me and My House: Crafting Your Marriage to Last* (Nashville, Tenn.: Thomas Nelson Publishers, 1987).

9. Paul Borgman, *Genesis: The Story We Haven't Heard* (Downers Grove, Ill.: InterVarsity Press, 2001), 117.

10. Sue Monk Kidd, *When the Heart Waits: Spiritual Direction for Life's Sacred Questions* (New York: HarperCollins, 1990), 123.

11. Steve Garber, *The Fabric of Faithfulness: Weaving Together Belief and Behavior during the University Years* (Downers Grove, Ill.: InterVarsity Press, 1996), 37.

12. Kidd, *When the Heart Waits*, 78.

13. Philip Yancey, *The Jesus I Never Knew* (Grand Rapids, Mich.: Zondervan, 1995), 36.

14. *United Methodist Hymnal* (Nashville, Tenn.: United Methodist Publishing House, 1989), 159.

# THE MATRIX OF VOCATION

*Burrell Dinkins*

KEEP US, LORD, SO AWAKE IN THE DUTIES OF OUR CALLINGS
THAT WE MAY SLEEP IN THY PEACE AND WAKE IN THY GLORY.
—JOHN DONNE

Paul Stevens defines ministry as "service to God" which is done "on behalf of God in the Church and the world."[1] To be "in ministry" does not necessarily imply being a paid staff member with a title and job description in the Church. Such professional ministers are, of course, the exception; most of us Christians serve God while seeking our livelihoods outside of the Church. Ministers are servant people, both laity and clergy, who put themselves at the disposal of God and the Church for service to God. A layperson working in a full-time "secular" vocation can be just as much in ministry as someone who works full-time in the Church.

I have made my livelihood mostly in the Church, as a missionary, pastor, counselor, and professor in theological seminaries. Each semester new seminarians come to campus to begin their first day of classes. As I look at their faces and hear their voices, I recall the prayer of one student, Joyce, as she began her seminary experience. Her words ring true for every Christian, no matter our individual vocation, career path, or level of education:

> Terrified—
> God, I am terrified,
>> And overwhelmed,
>> By the awesome responsibility
>> Of Your calling,
> The responsibility
>> For people's souls.
> When people come to me, God,
>> People in pain, wounded,
>> At their most vulnerable.
> Will I know how
>> To offer them Your healing,
>> To offer Your love?
> When people hear me speak,
>> Will they hear You?
>> Will it be Your message?
> Help me, God!
>> To learn all I can;
>> To grow all I can;
>> To listen, to discern.
> Help me, God!
>> You can heal the wounded;
>> You can speak through me.
> Only with You, God, can I fulfill your calling,
>> Can I bear this responsibility
>> Too awesome to be borne![2]

As Joyce reflected on her call, she saw that it was more than theological information. Her call was about the internal transformation. She understood the path before her to be one of responsibility, obedience, vulnerability, and loving service. This path meant to live in relationship with God and to accept God's calling with the awareness that this journey was beyond her own human power.

She depended upon the sustaining grace and power of the Holy Spirit to help her on her new journey. Joyce brought more than a good attitude to begin her theological education. She also brought a great deal of knowledge and wisdom from her years of experience in her former profession as a nursing educator. She did not need to leave behind what she had worked hard to learn but needed only to discover new ways to transform that knowledge into opportunities for theological reflection and service.

All of these traits of Joyce's journey should be true for every Christian. Each of us should be seeking God's internal transformation of our lives, humility to receive the Holy Spirit's power, and opportunities to use everything God has given us.

Some of my students have had definite calls to pastoral ministry and have run away from them like Jonah; some have had difficulty discerning their sense of vocation; others have had clear calls and have faithfully followed. The lives of my students have caused me to reflect upon *vocation*. To be called is very important, but to understand the nature and theology of vocation or calling is just as important.

A course that I teach on the vocation of ministry is the result of having thought long and hard on the essentials of understanding a call from God. After much prayer, reflection, and consultation from friends I have developed what I call the "matrix" of a call. When I use the word "matrix," I do not mean what the *Matrix* films mean as primarily a repressive force that surrounds and imprisons us, thus limiting our freedom and creativity. Morpheus's mission in the film is to find and train the One who will destroy the matrix and bring freedom to the human race.

In contrast to the destructive limitations of the film's matrix, I see the necessity of creating a new matrix that has the potential of containing and developing the essentials of the call to Christian service. Originally, "matrix" meant *mater*—the womb, source, origin, mother.

A matrix is the outer container holding something valuable that takes form and develops and without which it could not become what it was meant to be. I use the term here in the latter sense to indicate the *teleos* (perfect, complete end) of the call—the ultimate purpose and goal God intends. Like a magnet, the important parts of the call are held together into a meaningful whole, instead of spread out and separated into disconnected parts, thus losing the power of each one contributing to the other. I picture this matrix in the following way:

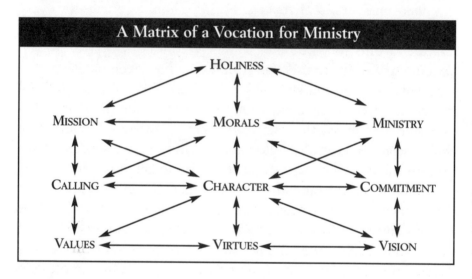

## A Matrix of a Vocation for Ministry

HOLINESS

MISSION    MORALS    MINISTRY

CALLING    CHARACTER    COMMITMENT

VALUES    VIRTUES    VISION

## Holiness

The various parts of the matrix of the call are linked together under the overarching framework of personal and social holiness. There is a direct link between a life of holiness and a life of ministry. One is not complete without the other. Personal and social holiness are the primary requisites for faithful service in the Church. Again and again, we encounter God's message in the Bible: "Be holy, because I am holy" (Lev. 19:2; 1 Pet. 1:15–16 NIV).

We cannot build a fruitful life of ministry without at the same time building a life of holiness. This happens when we draw near to God with a life of purity and allow God's sanctifying grace to penetrate every facet of our beings. Each point of the matrix depends upon this life of holiness. People eager to serve God also hunger for God. They want to know God as much as they want to serve God, even when they doubt they will completely fulfill the call to holiness.

*People eager to serve God also hunger for God.*

The matrix is designed to highlight the huge shift in consciousness that needs to take place to have a compelling and sustaining vision for the goodness and purity of God. The call to ministry requires a framework for holding together the essential elements of a life of ministry. Holiness is the linchpin that holds the various parts of the framework together. God does not impose it on us, but it is offered to us as a supernatural work of God's grace.

Holiness is more than a personal character trait. It also relates to a community of faith that is called to the practices of holiness. There are no individual saints. The word "saint" appears only in the plural in the New Testament. A life of holiness in an individual is formed by relationships within the community of saints. This process begins by the transformation of the system of values.

## Values

The construction of the matrix is based upon a firm foundation in values. Our values help us know what's important to us. They help guide us in our decisions and lead us to take responsibility for our actions. If we do not know what's important to us and what we stand for, our personal power degenerates into a confused and undirected life. On the other hand, when our values are transformed by Christ and by a daily life of holiness, we have a sense of purpose. The apostle Paul urged his readers to:

> offer your bodies as living sacrifices, holy and pleasing to God—this is your spiritual act of worship. Do not conform any longer to the pattern [values] of the world, but be transformed by the renewing of your mind. Then you will be able to test and approve what God's will is—his good, pleasing and perfect will. (Rom. 12:1–2 NIV)

A thorough examination of values is the first step in building a matrix strong enough to endure though a life of ministry. In my class on the vocation of ministry, students are asked to list their values at different stages in their lives. Many are surprised at how much they've changed because their values have been radically altered and their thinking has been transformed by their love for Christ. Biblical values have replaced secular values.

Although the term "values" is a relatively recent development, it is used rather loosely to mean the specific personal beliefs that help us decide what is important in life and where we should invest our energies and resources. They help direct our actions towards a particular kind of behavior.

Consciously or unconsciously, every decision or course of action is based in large part upon our values. Our values provide the "why" behind our specific actions. They help us make choices that direct our lives. Unfortunately, many Christian leaders do not stop to sort through and prioritize their values. Their ministry is not built upon clear Christian values. When they're confronted with a serious crisis, they are forced to stop and reexamine their values.

When I'm faced with tough decisions, I find it useful to consider my values and to seek guidance from them. While serving as missionaries in Brazil, my wife and I had little time to decide if we would hide Martha in our home from the military police. As the national president of the youth of our church, her crime was the illegal distribution of pamphlets petitioning the military government for free elections. Some of her student colleagues were imprisoned and tortured. Some of them died.

Martha and her fiancé managed to escape. She made her way to our house with only the clothes on her body. Trembling with fear for her life, she asked if she could stay in our home. My wife and I accepted the possibility that we could be discovered and jailed for hiding a fugitive from military justice. We also were concerned for the safety of our five children and the future of our work as missionaries.

Our values guided us in the choice to give Martha sanctuary and to protect her as if she were one of our own children. The risks were great, but our values were strong, even though we had to tell our children a lie as to the reason Martha had to live with us. During the year she was with us before we could help her escape to another country, our eldest daughter gave up her bed and slept on the couch in the living room. We even used deception to keep anyone from discovering her. Values founded upon the bedrock of love of God and neighbor guided our ethical decisions in a very difficult situation.

## Calling

When someone calls my name, I listen and look to find who is calling. In the Bible, "calling" and "caller" are closely linked together. Often the ones being called heard their names two times in succession before they answered the caller. This calling means there is a decisive and compelling appeal for all of our attention. Os Guinness defines Christian calling as "the truth that God calls us to himself so decisively that everything we are, everything we do, and everything we have is invested with a special devotion and dynamism lived out as a response to his summons and service."[3]

Many people have difficulty believing in divine guidance. Those who do believe tend to fall into Gordon Smith's three general categories of guidance. The first is the "blueprint" approach to guidance.

God is seen as having a perfect plan or blueprint for each person's life. The assumption here is that there is one perfect plan for each individual, and the goal of discernment is to discover this blueprint plan through observing specific signs.

*God is more interested in our availability than our ability.*

The second perspective is called "the wisdom school." Through reading Scripture and through praying, the mind is renewed to grow in wisdom about God's call. Instead of looking for signs as those of the blueprint school do, people trust their own capabilities in deciding what they are called to do.

I believe that most Christians can know the will of God for their lives; however, I'm skeptical in regards to people who casually say that God gives them specific instructions to follow. The blueprint followers too easily shift from one blueprint to another without constructing anything that lasts. The wisdom school followers depend too much on their own intelligence to figure out the direction for their lives.

Smith presents "friendship with God" as an alternative to the blueprint and the wisdom schools. This perspective begins with "a unique, personal and dynamic relationship with God; and it is from this relationship—not as servants, but as friends—that we encounter and respond to God and his will."[4] Through this dialogical friendship, ideas begin to emerge in our consciousness that we should give our lives or a major portion of our time in serving God. God most often speaks from the inside out, rather than through our ears.

God often speaks to us through other people, often from several persons over a period of time. Sometimes God calls persons through devotional readings, especially the Scripture. Some people report that God called them through service on mission trips where they were used by God to help alleviate suffering. Others hear God's call from significant nuclear experiences in their own lives, such as crisis and intense personal suffering. Additionally, a general sense of meaninglessness in one's daily work can lead to restlessness and a search for more significance in life through serving God and others. When all else fails, God may use extra-ordinary means to call a person to specific roles and tasks. Many of these extraordinary experiences are recorded in the Scriptures.

What is important is not the means, however ordinary or extraordinary. That we hear God's call and respond to it in appro-priate ways is what is important. God is more interested in our *availability* than our *ability* to do specific kinds of ministry. Uniqueness of the various calls to ministry is much more impor-tant than reading the patterns of the call.

## Mission

I am the person I am today as a result of mission. When I was a boy, my family attended a mission church started by the Methodists in Valdosta, Georgia. The congregation grew until it became a strong church with a vibrant youth program. I made my profession of faith, grew in my Christian commitment, and received a call to full-time Christian ministry in this church. I am a product of the missionary activity of the Church. I'm now a participant in God's mission activity as one who has been sent by the Sender.

Mission begins as the overflow of God's love in creating, sustaining, and renewing the universe. So, mission is joining God in His caring, sustaining, and transforming activity on earth.[5] Mission is more than the activity of the Church, or some mission agency performing under the imperatives of the Great Commission, or even as appreciation for what God has done for us. It is an expression of God's concern for the world. I responded to the invitation to participate, not from the pressing needs of the people in Brazil, but from a calling and sending God. Jesus said, "As the Father has sent me, I am sending you" (John 20:21; cf. 17:18 NIV).

The Church's mission is to discover what God is doing in the world, celebrate God's activity, and find out how to participate in it. Just as there is no calling without a caller, neither is there a sending in mission without a sender. Both a calling and a sending require a responder. The prophet Isaiah heard the call in the temple: "Whom shall I send? And who will go for us?" His immediate response was, "Here am I. Send me" (Isa. 6:8 NIV)!

The sending God is also an accompanying God to sustain the mission "goer." We see this fact in the Great Commission:

> Then Jesus came to them and said, "All authority in heaven and on earth has been given to me. Therefore go and make disciples of all nations, baptizing them in the name of the Father and of the Son and of the Holy Spirit, and teaching them to obey everything I have commanded you. And surely I am with you always, to the very end of the age." (Matt. 28:18–20 NIV)

## Virtues

Our language is not sufficient for conveying a full understanding of the nature of virtue. In its original meaning in the Greek language, "virtue" is the power to do that which something was created to do. The virtue of the eye is the power to see. The kind of virtue I'm concerned about here is moral virtue. This is the excellence of character that helps us fulfill and protect our calling as Christian disciples.

A virtue is an acquired excellence of the soul. It is the most enduring legacy of our lives. It is the qualities of lives that could be related in our funeral eulogies, and people who knew us would agree that the words are true to the way we lived our lives.

Virtues are different from gifts or talents; virtues are acquired through repeated practice of certain habits over an extended amount of time and through effort until they become second nature. From a Wesleyan perspective, virtues are created and developed by the cooperative action of both the Holy Spirit and the person practicing the virtues in Christian community. God's grace is necessary; nevertheless, both time and effort are required for virtues to become deep and lasting qualities. Virtues guide our behavior towards right actions whether or not there are rules to govern the behavior.

Virtues go beyond skills, though skills may have some of the same features in their manner of acquisition. A virtuous person needs skills in order to effectively practice the virtues. For eight years I lived behind a college baseball field. Sometimes I watched the players practice over and over the same set of plays until they became second nature to them. They were developing playing skills. Virtue goes beyond these in that a virtuous player would be one who was highly motivated to practice in order to become the best player possible according to his own set of values and the common values of the team.

Virtue is directly related to motivation that initiates and directs our actions to produce anticipated results. Motivation is a deep part of a person's character that provides guidance for what to do in the daily circumstances of life in terms of the end and means that underlie our actions. A person motivated by the virtue of love will act for the overall good of another person. A person motivated by vices or lust will act in a vicious manner to satisfy those desires. Jesus said:

> *The good man brings good things out of the good stored up in his heart, and the evil man brings evil things out of the evil stored up in the heart. For out of the overflow of his heart his mouth speaks. (Luke 6:45 NIV)*

The practice of the virtues leads to a virtuous life. The practice of vices leads to a vicious life. The apostle Paul gives a clear distinction between a vice-filled life and a life of virtue in Galatians 5. He contrasts the Christian life as a life of virtue lived under the guidance of the Holy Spirit and a life of vice lived counter to the Spirit. He used an agricultural metaphor to describe the virtues by calling them the fruit of the Spirit: love, joy, peace, patience, kindness, goodness, faithfulness, gentleness, and self-control. Then he says that the motivation for using these virtues goes beyond the commands of the law, the rules that control behavior.

All of this leads us to the conclusion that virtues are deep and enduring traits acquired through the grace of God and our own active participation. Virtues reveal the excellence of a person that comes from a motivation to produce good behavior. The practice of virtue implies the development of habits to do what is right because it is best for others and it comes from the depth of our hearts.

> *The practice of the virtues leads to a virtuous life. The practice of vices leads to a vicious life.*

Eric Liddell, a young Scottish missionary whose story is told in the film *Chariots of Fire*, plans to return to China, but first is seeking to glorify God in his body by running for the gold medal in the Olympics. Eric's sister tries to persuade him to return immediately to his mission work. He replies, "I believe God made me for a purpose [i.e., China]. But He also made me fast, and when I run I feel His pleasure." When we train ourselves in moral virtue, *arête*, we feel His pleasure (and power). God empowers us for that which we were created to become.

## Character

Many years ago public schools used to post the following verse:

Be careful of your thoughts,
For your thoughts become your words;
Be careful of your words,
For your words become your deeds;

Be careful of your deeds,
For your deeds become your habits;
Be careful of your habits,
For your habits become your character;
Be careful of your character,
For your character becomes your destiny.[6]

For several decades words like these disappeared from North American education; but one of the most important developments in recent times is the renewal of interest in, and concern for, character formation. Usually this means character development without religion or foundational principles.

The media is filled with stories about leaders whose failures demonstrate problems with character. Each year over 80 million lawsuits are filed in the United States—152 lawsuits every minute in the year. One reason for so many lawsuits is that even though the United States has less than 6 percent of the world's population, the U.S. has 70 percent of the world's lawyers, with over five hundred thousand students in law schools.[7]

Another reason is the neglect of character formation. A crisis in character formation leads to the creation of more and more laws, or to a general breakdown into lawlessness. Os Guinness writes:

> Externally, character provides the point of trust that links leaders with followers; internally, character is the part-gyroscope, part-brake that provides the leader's strongest source of bearings and restraint. In many instances the first prompting to do good and the last barrier against doing wrong are the same—character.[8]

Character is that which regulates our responses to actual or anticipated pleasure or pain. Character is the core of a person. Guinness writes, "Character, as rooted in the Greek word for the graphic device depicting a hallmark or distinguishing sign [i.e., *icon*], stamps a person decisively beneath all masks, poses, disguises, and social veneers."9 People of character are people of principles; and strength of character can help us keep our integrity through tough ethical situations.

As Christian disciples we are responsible not only for our actions but also for our character because, over time, character is shaped by accumulated habits of the heart and decisions we make on a daily basis. We constantly create a narrative of our lives with the plot centered in our character. Like it or not, we are always "in character."

The good news is that we are not alone. The work of character formation depends upon the sanctifying grace of God; it also depends upon our response to that grace through our participation in the means and practices of a life of personal and social holiness. The habits of virtue contribute to the habits of the heart. To cultivate these habits we need to pray the prayer of David: "Search me, O God, and know my heart [character] . . . See if there is any offensive way [vice] in me" (Ps. 139:23–24 NIV).

## Morals

Morality is a set of norms that form how we live our lives. These are directly related to our values, character, and the virtues that support them. As Christians we are called to live in a way that supports what we have learned as Christ's disciples. Our source of morality is taken from understanding God's Word, will, and call.

The word "moral" comes from the Latin word *mos*, which means custom or habit (virtue). A moral person examines proposed action in light of his/her integrity. A moral person checks first to discover what is good for the others as well as oneself. Morality goes beyond what is legal in that public law often does not give guidance for proper Christian behavior; and at times morality even may counter supporting oppressive governmental laws.

One notable quality of human nature is to promote our own perceived good; but to be morally good, humans need both constraints to control using others for selfish ends and motivations to do good for others. The good of the whole needs to be looked at when considering right behavior. Frequently, the standards for morality are beyond our human desires and natural capacities; therefore, we need outside assistance to help us choose that which is good. If we pretend we have the capacity to be morally good without God's assistance, we will fail. If we recognize the high demands of morality but rationalize by lowering our standards to meet out natural ability, we will fail to become moral persons. When we look for substitutes for God's grace to maintain moral standards, we fall into a moral gap and fail to live up to our values.

One difference between the virtuous person and the moral person is that the latter is able to overcome temptation only in those situations where she knows the right thing to do and is motivated to do it. The virtuous person has acquired the habit of feeling as well as acting. She has developed a habit of being motivated in a certain way and is not as subject to the same temptations as the moral person. A virtuous Christian is motivated to choose rightly from within and from without through the grace of God.

The moral life is directly related to how a person lives in community with others. Morality is taught, encouraged, and sustained by the community of faith. Moral failures need community discipline. Moreover, morality shapes one's relationship with God, with one's self, and with the community of faith. Having received faith, one becomes faithful through the practice of virtues until they become internal motivations to live a Christian moral life. Faithfulness to God and the practice of personal integrity affects and guides one's moral life. Faithful moral living is an intellectual, emotional, and spiritual affirmation that what one believes one also practices.

## Vision

Calling begins with God's vision for redeeming the world. "God so loved the world that he gave his one and only Son, that whoever believes in him shall not perish" (John 3:16 NIV). Our calling comes from God's vision for a better world. To participate in this vision we need to become visionary persons.

Far too few called to ministry have a clear vision of what they are to do with their lives. Vision is like planning a trip. We need to know where we want to go before we start the journey. Vision is a signpost pointing the way towards a future that is very important, realistic, attractive, and something that generates passionate participation.

Vision begins as only an idea or image that builds motivational energy to use all our resources to arrive at the place we envision. Steve Jobs's vision of a personal desktop computer led him and others to invest time, energy, and money in the development and marketing of the Macintosh computers. Martin Luther King's vision of racial equality articulated in his famous "I Have a Dream" speech in Washington, D.C., inspired the passage of the Civil Rights Bill in the U.S. Congress.

I require my students to write and often rewrite several times their vision for ministry. In their first drafts most of them confuse their vision statement with their mission statement. A good vision statement creates a clear picture of where they want their Christian life and ministry to be in five, ten, fifteen, or more years in the future. An unclear vision statement is like an unclear windshield that creates anxiety about what is ahead and makes driving dangerous. Though the future is unknown and unpredictable, it is worth the pain of disappointment to look to the future—something that exists only in the mind and spirit's eye—to participate in creating that which we are to become by the grace of God.

Vision has served me well. It has inspired me to

> *Vision is like planning a trip. We need to know where we want to go before we start the journey.*

achieve much more than I dreamed possible. It gave me something to aspire to and it caused others to help me realize the vision. It helped me jump-start my future and propelled me towards my goals. Rearview mirrors are very important because they help us see what is behind us, but the front windshield is far more important because it helps us get a picture of where we're going. Vision is both seeing and living by faith.

## Commitments

The initial call to ministry begins when we respond to the call that Jesus gave His first disciples: "Come, follow me" (Matt. 4:19 NIV). How we respond to this call is an important test of our values because we become that to which we are committed. Commitment restricts, as well as disciplines, the freedom to act. No longer are we our own. We belong to Him. How we fulfill this commitment is also an important test of character because commitment means seeing something through to completion despite difficulties. Spiritual growth is not automatic. It requires an intentional commitment to grow in our discipleship to Jesus Christ.

As part of our commitment in community, my wife and I belong to a small group from our church. It's refreshing to be with Christian friends committed to growing in devotion to Christ and service to others. After a discussion about prayer we joined hands to pray and heard Tommy say that he had never prayed out loud in front of other people. The leader shared how difficult it was for her the first time she prayed in front of others. She invited Tommy to try and he did, much to the joy of his spiritual companions.

Nothing shapes our lives more than the commitments we make. Our commitments can make us stronger, or they can destroy us. This is why many of us are hesitant to make commitments. We prefer the anxiety of drifting through life rather than the fear of making a wrong commitment. Others commit only to easy tasks to avoid disappointment but find only mediocrity.

The purpose of a call is to help us make the decision to follow Christ regardless of the cost of discipleship. The initial stage is usually filled with joy and excitement, but soon the hardships come. This is when it is difficult to remain faithful to our commitments.

This is why vows are often used to seal the commitment. They are somewhat like business contracts, except they are verbal rather than written agreements between two or more parties. Church membership vows and wedding vows are covenant commitments that bind the two parties to fulfill them.

When I became a Christian, my first commitment was to study the Bible and learn as much about the story of God as possible. I also started tithing my salary to the Church and serving the needs of others in the community. I was highly committed to live my faith in every area of my life. My values changed. Though it was difficult at first, I practiced the Christian virtues and struggled to develop a Christian character. When I was first called to the ordained ministry, I made a commitment to attend seminary in order to become the most effective pastor possible.

Sometimes commitment is costly. To be committed also means a willingness to be unhappy for a while. Sacrifices often are required in a committed life. A person unwilling to make the sacrifices necessary to endure tough times will not enjoy the rewards of the good times.

Commitment to the call of God means to be dedicated towards fulfilling that call and "to live a life worthy of the calling you have received" (Eph. 4:1 NIV). This dedication motivates us to move forward in the path we have chosen. Dedication also implies restraints upon endangering the fulfillment of the call through entering other commitments or crossing boundaries that would compromise that fulfillment.

## Ministry

Jesus came to seek and save the lost through ministry, or service, to them. He modeled servanthood to His disciples by reversing the usual relationship between master and disciple when He took on the role of a slave and washed the feet of the disciples. He wanted them to understand that as His followers they are to live a life of service. They are not to seek position, title, economic advantages, or prestige; rather, the character of their lives is to be like His—a servant. The whole people of God are in the ministry. Ministry pleases God because it is done to and for Him for the sake of the world.

My brother and sister-in-law invited my wife and me to eat lunch at a local restaurant close to their home. The waitress introduced herself and took our order with all the courtesy of a host in her home. She brought our meals and carefully arranged them on our table. When she was satisfied she stepped back and asked, "Is there anything missing or something else I can do to help you enjoy your meal?"

I said to her, "One thing is missing. We need to say grace before eating this food that you have served us. Would you say grace for us?"

Without blinking an eye she responded, "Sure. I'll be glad to do that if you will all join hands before we pray." Then she prayed a beautiful prayer of blessings for us and for our food.

When she left, my brother asked how I knew she was a Christian. I responded that she had to be because her service was an act of ministry.

He said he was going to have to pay more for the tip. I said she deserved it because she served us a Christian ministry.

Before we left I thanked her for her ministry, and I was filled with joy. Another faithful person had answered the call!

**NOTES**

1. R. Paul Stevens, *The Other Six Days* (Grand Rapids, Mich.: Eerdmans/Regent College, 1999), 133.

2. Joyce Alexander, unpublished class paper.

3. Os Guinness, *The Call* (Nashville, Tenn.: W. Publishing Group, 2003), 4.

4. Gordon T. Smith, *Alone with the Lord: A Guide to a Personal Day of Prayer* (Vancouver, B.C.: Regent College Publishing, 2003), 24–25.

5. Howard A. Snyder, "Mission," *The Complete Book of Everyday Christianity*, ed. Robert Banks and R. Paul Stevens (Downers Grove, Ill.: InterVarsity Press, 1997), 645–50.

6. John Law, "Be Careful," n.p., n.d.

7. *Orlando Sentinel*, October 5, 2003.

8. Guinness, *The Call*, 20.

9. Ibid., 12.

# THE MESSAGE OF THE MASTER AND THE CONTENT OF OUR CALLING: "A NEW THING"—ISAIAH 43

*Sandra Richter*

THEREFORE, I URGE YOU, BROTHERS, IN VIEW OF GOD'S MERCY, TO OFFER YOUR BODIES AS LIVING SACRIFICES, HOLY AND PLEASING TO GOD—THIS IS YOUR SPIRITUAL ACT OF WORSHIP.

—ROMANS 12:1 NIV

One thing that should energize a Christian is a testimony of God's grace. We should never tire of hearing how God has rescued yet another broken life from the consequences of sin. After all, grace is at the heart of what our faith is about. Certainly it is appropriate that a Christian would be inspired by such testimony, because the recitation of the mighty acts of God is the substance of the record of redemptive history—what we know as the Bible. One particular passage of this sacred record speaks to the content of our calling as Christians: the magnificent oracle of the prophet Isaiah in chapter 43 of the book that bears his name.

The oracle is located in what is known as "Second Isaiah," chapters 40 through 66. What distinguishes the second half of Isaiah's book from the first is the shift in message. Whereas

First Isaiah focuses on the sin of Israel (giving a painfully detailed description of how this nation's unremitting rebellion had resulted in her ultimate rejection and demise), the second half is replete with the message of the restoration of this same group of people. Thus, with most of the first half of Isaiah's book directed toward the citizens of independent, pre-exilic Jerusalem during the late eighth century BC, most of the second half is directed toward the survivors of the capture of Jerusalem by the Neo-Babylonian empire in 586 BC, the citizens of the Exile. The book makes a major shift at chapter 40: whereas chapters 1 through 39 focus upon the "former things" (the description of Israel as she was), the second half focuses upon the "latter things" (a description of Israel as she would be). Chapters 40 to 43 serve as the introduction to these latter things, and our oracle, chapter 43, is the climax of that introduction.

> But now, thus says Yahweh, your creator oh Jacob,
> and your designer oh Israel.
> Do not fear, because I have redeemed you,
> I have called you by my name, you are mine.
> When you cross through the waters, I will be with you,
> and through the rivers, they will not overflow you.
> When you go into the midst of the fire, you will not be burned,
> and the flame will not kindle upon you.
> Because I, Yahweh, am your God;
> the Holy one of Israel is your deliverer.
> I have given Egypt (as) your ransom,
> Cush and Seba instead of you.
> Because you are precious in my eyes,
> you are honored and I love you,
> I will give a person in your place,
> and peoples in exchange for your life.
> Do not fear, for I am with you. (Isa. 43:1–5a)[1]

*From the East I will bring your offspring,*
*and from the West I will gather you.*
*I will say to the North, "Give (them) up!"*
*and to the South, "Do not keep (them) imprisoned!"*
*Bring forth my sons from a distance,*
*my daughters from the edges of the earth,*
*all the ones called by my name,*
*and whom I have created for my glory, whom I have fashioned,*
*even whom I have made . . . (Isa. 43:5b–7)*

———

*Do not remember the former things, or ponder things of the past.*
*At this moment, I am doing a new thing,*
*now it will spring forth, will you not recognize it?*
*Indeed, I will place a highway in the wilderness, rivers in the desert.*
*The beast(s) of the field will glorify me, the jackals and ostriches*
*for I have put water in the wilderness, rivers in the desert,*
*in order to give drink to my chosen people,*
*(in order that) this people whom I have designed for myself,*
*might recount my praise! (Isa. 43:18–21)*

As we consider this oracle, the first question we encounter is from what is Israel being redeemed (v. 1)? The answer has to do with the exilic stage of Israel's story. At this point in her history, Israel is looking back on the most horrific judgment that the nation had ever experienced, the conquest of Judah by Nebuchadnezzar II and the deportation of the entire populace to the distant city of Babylon. After years of warnings by means of His servants, the prophets—sermon after sermon, oracle after oracle, myriads of "second chances"—Yahweh had at last fulfilled the covenant curse. The God of Israel had sent the armies of Babylonia to wipe out the cities of Judah, raze Jerusalem, and drag off the survivors as slaves and exiles to a land they had not known, nearly twelve hundred miles away.

In this devastation, the people of Judah lost everything. Certainly their homes and their wealth but also their families, their friends, and their positions in society. Thousands perished, and those who survived were exiled, tied together, and driven before the armies of the greatest military power of that age. They brought with them the clothes on their backs, perhaps a small wagon of possessions, a goat, or a cow. We will never know how many died along the way.

These citizens of Israel lost their homeland, their identity, their temple, and the ability to practice their religion. The result? A broken people, a broken covenant, a broken dream.

Why had these people been so severely judged? The answer may be found at Mt. Sinai. Here Yahweh had promised Israel that if they kept His covenant they would keep the land. Moreover, He had promised them as their suzerain lord that He would give to them "great and splendid cities which you did not build, and houses full of all good things which you did not fill, and hewn cisterns which you did not dig, vineyards and olive trees which you did not plant" (Deut. 6:10–11 NASB). Yahweh promised them that He would defend them against foreign oppression and that He would dwell in their midst, first in the tabernacle and eventually in the temple at Jerusalem. From the perspective of a landless, nomadic people, whose most recent memory was seemingly unending years of slavery, Israel had been given paradise.

But Yahweh had also promised them that if they broke covenant, they would be driven from this land. The covenant was clear—all of these good gifts were dependent upon the nation maintaining its commitment to God. The demands were minimal, but they were not negotiable.

Hence, after generations of prophetic warning and protest, at last the axe fell. Israel was guilty. As the prophet catalogues throughout the first half of his book: Israel had again and again chosen wealth over justice, popularity over integrity, religiosity over piety, self-indulgence over self-sacrifice, the honor of men over the honor of God. As Isaiah's very first oracle summarizes,

Yahweh was left in the position of asking the question: Where will you be stricken again, where can you add to your apostasy? I have disciplined you in every possible way, and *still* you rebel. What is left to do (Isa. 1:1–9)?

What was left to do? To enact the covenant curse. And so Israel was stripped of hearth and home, life and offspring, temple and nation. A broken covenant resulted in a broken people and a broken dream. Who had brought this curse upon Israel? Who had so crushed God's people? The answer is in the introduction to our oracle (42:24–25). *Yahweh* had judged His people, because His people were guilty.

But one of the astonishing things about the character of this God whom we serve is that judgment is never the entirety of His plan. Rather, after bringing this judgment upon His people (a judgment well deserved), Yahweh speaks through His prophet the message of restoration. What will this restoration look like for Israel? A *return* from the exile to which their sin and rebellion had driven them.

And, thus, we answer our first question: From what was Israel being redeemed? From the consequences of her own sin. With that question answered, let us consider the rest of the words of the prophet Isaiah.

> But now, thus says Yahweh, your creator oh Jacob,
> and your designer oh Israel.
> Do not fear, because I have redeemed you,
> I have called you by my name, you are mine. (Isa. 43:1)

Even in their wretchedness, Israel is not disowned. Yahweh is not afraid to claim these people as His own. Rather, the God of Israel shouts out for all to hear: "Do not fear, I have redeemed you!" Let us not read this passage too quickly. Because here we encounter a very ancient concept, the concept of "redemption."

Most assume that this is a holy word, designed specifically for theological discourse. But in reality, the idea of redemption began in a completely secular context; specifically, it arises from the tribal laws of Israel's earliest experiences. The concept is built upon the responsibility of the patriarch of a clan toward the members of his extended family. Within the ancient tribal culture from which Israel emerged, the ties of blood were stronger than life, and the patriarch of the clan was the one upon whom the authority and responsibility for maintaining the well-being of the clan rested. Hence, one aspect of the tribal law of redemption was the patriarch's responsibility to ransom a family member who had been captured as a prisoner of war and/or had been sold into slavery.

*In reality, the idea of redemption began in a completely secular context.*

In this oracle, Yahweh steps into the role of the faithful patriarch. He will pay whatever price is demanded for His rebellious child. Although Israel's present captive state is clearly her own doing, rather than abandoning this sad excuse for "a holy nation," Yahweh instead declares that He will pay the ransom demanded; He will buy them back from the strong enemy who has imprisoned them. And even though the road home will be very difficult, dangerous, and frightening . . .

> *When you cross through the waters, I will be with you,*
> *and through the rivers, they will not overflow you.*
> *When you go into the midst of the fire, you will not be burned,*
> *and the flame will not kindle upon you.*
> *Because I, Yahweh, am your God;*
> *the Holy one of Israel is your deliverer.*
> *I have given Egypt (as) your ransom,*
> *Cush and Seba instead of you.*
> *Because you are precious in my eyes,*
> *you are honored and I love you,*

*I will give a person in your place,*
*and peoples in exchange for your life.*
*Do not fear, for I am with you. (Isa. 43:2–5a)*

In the introduction to this oracle we read that Yahweh "poured out on him the heat of his anger and the fierceness of battle, and it set him aflame all around . . ." But now we read, "when you walk through the fire, I will not let it burn you." Yes, Israel's road home will be extremely difficult; there will be fire and flood.

But God is promising them that He will not allow these terrors to overcome them. Rather, Yahweh states that He Himself will go before them. "For I am with you." Let me say that again, "for I am with you." The long journey home will be one that Israel will not walk alone. Moreover, the *world* will know that this once-humiliated band of Babylonian exiles are nothing less than the possession of the most high God, because Yahweh will go *with them*.

Remember that this statement is made to a people whose theology was founded on the idea of the presence of God. The entire premise behind the existence of the tabernacle and temple was to facilitate the dwelling of God in the midst of the nation of Israel (Exod. 25:8—"Let them build a sanctuary for me *so that* I may dwell among them.").

*As far as these folks knew, Yahweh had no intention of ever returning.*

In the judgment and the collapse of the monarchy, the temple had been razed and the presence of God had departed. As far as these folks knew, Yahweh had no intention of ever returning. Yet this message from the second half of Isaiah declares: "I am *with* you."

The climax of this oracle (which is the climax of the introduction to the latter things) is verses 5 through 7. Spoken to a
nation whose people had first been scattered to the far reaches of
the North in 722 BC when the northern kingdom fell and then to
the East in 586 BC when the southern kingdom fell, Yahweh says:
"I will bring you home."

> From the East I will bring your offspring,
> and from the West I will gather you.
> I will say to the North, "Give (them) up!"
> and to the South, "Do not keep (them) imprisoned!"
> Bring forth my sons from a distance,
> my daughters from the edges of the earth,
> all the ones called by my name,
> and whom I have created for my glory,
> whom I have fashioned,
> even whom I have made . . .(Isa. 43:5b–7)

As the oracle continues, we learn that as a result of Israel's
restoration, Israel who was *blind* will now stand as a *witness* to
the nations (vv. 8–13). How could a blind person serve as a
witness? Isaiah tells us that first Israel herself will be healed of
her own blindness—she will finally understand who it is that she
has been serving. And then the *nations*, seeing Israel's miraculous
deliverance, will come to understand who it is Israel has been
serving as well.

What will Israel and the nations come to understand? "It is I
who have declared and saved and proclaimed, and there was no
strange god among you" (v. 12)! And just as Yahweh defeated the
Egyptians who held His people in bondage so many generations
before, so shall Yahweh defeat the Babylonians who hold His
people in bondage now (vv. 14–17).

Lastly, the prophet exhorts Israel to forget its past and to gaze
with faith into the future.

*Do not remember the former things, or ponder things of the past.*
*At this moment, I am doing a new thing,*
*now it will spring forth, will you not recognize it?*
*Indeed, I will place a highway in the wilderness, rivers in the desert.*
*The beast(s) of the field will glorify me, the jackals and ostriches*
*for I have put water in the wilderness, rivers in the desert,*
*in order to give drink to my chosen people,*
*(in order that) this people whom I have designed for myself,*
*might recount my praise! (Isa. 43:18–21)*

Note the final verse. The *goal* of this redemptive act is that "this people whom I have designed myself" might recount Yahweh's praise. This point requires us to pause and to focus. The prophet Isaiah is telling us that the ultimate objective of God's saving acts on Israel's behalf is that a testimony of these acts might go forth to the nations. In other words, *it is by means of the testimony of those whose lives have been restored by Yahweh's miraculous grace that the nations will learn of the God of Israel.*

And what of this "new thing"? Certainly the miraculous restoration of the Jews to their homeland is the immediate context of this prophecy. Although we know of many people groups who were exiled over the decades of the Assyrian and Babylonian empires, we have only *one* story of a people who returned to their homeland and resurrected a life long dead.

The fact that a power shift in international politics (the Medo-Persian Empire's successful conquest of the Babylonian Empire) could result in a new policy regarding exiled people groups (the Edict of Cyrus in 538 BC that freed all the exiles of the Persian Empire to return to their homelands) is miracle enough. But the fact that there were Jews who were willing to leave Babylon is additionally amazing. In the seventy years of Judah's exile, the Judeans had learned a new language, established new businesses, and built new homes. They and their children had been assimilated into Babylonian culture. Moreover, by the time of Cyrus's decree, only those who had been small children at the time of the deportation had any living memory of Judah. Asking the typical Jew in Babylon in 538 BC if he or she wanted to "go home," would have been equivalent to asking my father (an officer in the U.S. Navy) if he wanted to go home to Russia, the last citizenship of his father prior to his immigration to the United States. I assure you, just as my father considered the United States his home, so would the typical exiled Judean in Babylon.

In addition to the realities of cultural assimilation in Babylon, another deterring factor to the whole-scale return of the Judeans was the recasting of Israelite religion during the exilic period. During the exile, the expatriates from Judah recreated their religion in a way that it could be practiced a world away from the now-demolished temple. This new form of Israelite religion is what we have come to know as Judaism and was centered around the synagogue and the Torah as opposed to the priesthood and the temple. Thus, much of the motivation for going home had been resolved well before the Edict of Cyrus.

In light of this, the fact that there were Jews who *would* leave is amazing in and of itself. But when we realize that those who dared to return managed to rebuild their community from the ruins of war-torn Palestine—to rebuild their city and their temple, reestablish their priesthood, and reexperience the prophetic office—the only word that can apply to this restoration of the Jewish community is "miraculous."

But even with this truly miraculous restoration, we find that much of the promised redemption of Israel seems to remain undone. When we consider that the population of the restored community of Israel has been estimated at less than a third of the size of pre-exilic Judah (some would say less than a tenth), we realize that *most* of the Babylonian Jews did *not* return. Moreover, our knowledge of international politics in this era tells us that for those who did, they returned as citizens of another nation. Judah was now a Persian province, nothing more. The glory of the Davidic monarchy, the Solomonic temple, and the

Abrahamic boundaries of Israel had become a thing of the distant, and apparently unrecoverable, past. And the settlers were not unaware of this reality. No, for the Jew, although the restoration of Isaiah's oracle *began* in 538 BC with Cyrus's decree, this restoration did not end there.

In Ezekiel 37:21–28, we get a full picture of the hope of the Jew.

*Say to them, "Thus says my lord, Yahweh, 'I will take the sons of Israel from among the nations where they have gone, and I will gather them from every side and bring them into their own land; and I will make them one nation in the land, on the mountains of Israel; and one king will be king for all of them; and they will no longer be two nations and no longer be divided into two kingdoms. They will no longer defile themselves with their idols, or with their detestable things, or with any of their transgressions; but I will deliver them from all their backslidings in which they have sinned, and will cleanse them. And they will be my people, and I will be their God. My servant David will be king over them, and they will all have one shepherd; and they will walk in my ordinances and keep my statutes and observe them. They will live on the land that I gave to Jacob my servant, in which your fathers lived; and they will live on it, they, and their sons and their sons' sons, forever; and David my servant will be their prince forever. I will make a covenant of peace with them; it will be an everlasting covenant with them. And I will place them and multiply them, and will set my sanctuary in their midst forever. My dwelling place also will be with them; and I will be their God, and they will be my people. And the nations will know that I am Yahweh, the one who sanctifies Israel, when my sanctuary is in their midst forever.'"*

Nehemiah is still echoing this dream as he prepares to lead the last of the three groups of returnees from Babylon. He prays:

*Remember the word which you commanded your servant Moses, saying, "If you are unfaithful, I will scatter you among the peoples, but if you will*

*return to me and keep my commandments and do them, (even) if your scat-*
*tered ones are at the edge of heaven, from there I will gather them, and I*
*will bring them to the place in which I chose to place my name." (Neh. 1:9)*

So even after the main corps of Judeans had *already* returned to Palestine, Nehemiah continues to speak of the dream of "gathering" the scattered ones, *restoring* the nation.

Space does not permit me to discuss the various testimonies to this not-yet-fulfilled expectation of the Jews. But the literature of the post-exilic and intertestamental periods is replete with messages regarding the regathering of the "exiles" (Zech. 10:6–10; 2 Macc. 1:27–29, 2:17–18; Bar. 4:37, 5:55; Song of Sol. 17:21–32; the Book of Jubilees 1:15).

The authors of the "Rule of the Community" (a text belonging to the corpus of the Dead Sea Scrolls and dating within a hundred years of Jesus), *still* speak of themselves as "captives." In sum, this post-exilic and intertestamental literature makes it very clear that from the perspective of the Jews, the true restoration of the nation, the new thing of Isaiah's oracle, had not yet come.

This brings us at last to the New Testament. And we are struck by the fact that all four gospel writers introduce their accounts of the ministry of Jesus with the same figure: John the Baptist. It is an unusual thing to be able to say that Matthew, Mark, Luke, *and* John use the same motif in the same manner. Their individual styles and theological agendas usually result in unique arrangements of their material. But apparently the message of John the Baptist is of such dramatic importance that each of these men, under the inspiration of the Holy Spirit, chose him and his message to introduce the ministry of Jesus.

Moreover, all of the gospel writers describe John in the very same way: "This is the one referred to by Isaiah the prophet, saying: 'The voice of one crying in the wilderness, make ready the way of the Lord, make his paths straight!'" (Matt 3:3; cf. Mark 1:1–4, Luke 3:3–6, John 1:6–23 NASB). You will notice that the gospel writers are all quoting a single text: Isaiah 40:3, the opening chapter of Isaiah's restoration oracles. This is Isaiah's first word on the latter things; it is also the introduction to our oracle, Isaiah 43.

Of what is Isaiah speaking when he cries out "make ready the way of the Lord"? He is speaking metaphorically of the international highway required for Yahweh to lead the exiles home from Babylon! And what are the gospel writers telling us by quoting Isaiah's opening oracle on the restoration? Why does this passage from Isaiah have such a prominent position in the gospel story? Because the gospel writers want to make very sure that we are clear that the new thing that Isaiah was preaching, the *true* restoration of the nation of Israel, is about to begin! But this time, the one who will "lead captive a host of captives" is Yahweh, the Son—Jesus, the deliverer.

> *The new thing that Isaiah was preaching, the true restoration of the nation of Israel, is about to begin.*

Consider the words of John 11:47–52. Here at the end of John's gospel, as the Passion week is about to begin, we read:

> Therefore the chief priests and the Pharisees convened a council, and were saying, "What are we doing? For this man is performing many signs. If we let Him go on like this, all men will believe in Him, and the Romans will come and take away both our place and our nation." But one of them, Caiaphas, who was high priest that year, said to them, "You know nothing at all, nor do you take into account that it is expedient for you that one man die for the people, and that the whole nation not perish." Now he did not say this on his own initiative, but being high priest that year, he prophesied that Jesus was going to die for the nation, and not for the nation only, but in order that He might also gather together into one the children of God who are scattered abroad. (NASB)

Yes, the restoration about which Isaiah so compellingly preaches does indeed speak of the Babylonian Judeans who dared to return. Those who, although surely frightened by the long road ahead and fearful of what they would find when they finally reached Palestine, dared to believe the word of the prophet and come home. But as the Jews of Jesus' day were well aware, there were still many Jewish exiles scattered throughout the land who needed to be brought home. You can hear this assumption in the narrator's words: "that he might also gather together into one the children of God who are scattered abroad."

But what the Jews of Jesus' day struggled to understand is that Yahweh would not be satisfied with simply bringing home the exiles of Israel. No, Isaiah's oracle had a much broader purview than the Judeans could have imagined. And what the gospel writers are telling us in introducing the ministry of the Christ by quoting Isaiah is that Jesus' mission was to, at last, fully accomplish the new thing. And what was this new thing? Nothing less than the impossible idea that not only could the exiles of Judah come home, *but the exiles of Eden could come home as well.*

Jesus said: "But I have other sheep, which are not of this fold; I must bring them also, and they will hear my voice; and they will become one flock with one shepherd" (John 10:16 NASB). His disciples did not understand that Jesus was speaking of people *other* than the children of Abraham.

Paul said: "If one is in Christ, there is a new creation; the old has passed away, behold, the new (thing) has come" (2 Cor. 5:17). But we do not understand that Paul is using the motif of Israel's story to tell us our own. The Scriptures are clear that the mission of the Messiah was to bring the exiles home. But you and I stand here today as a testimony to the fact that the lost daughters and sons whom Jesus came to call home were not all Jews. Rather, Jesus came so that every tongue, tribe, and nation could hear the amazing message that although our sin resulted in our exile, drove us to the very edge of heaven, left us in a place where we were sure that God had forgotten us . . . Yahweh has announced that now we can come home. And even though we are guilty, filthy, and unworthy of His concern, our Creator, the One who formed us, cries out through the voice of the prophet: "Do not be afraid, I have redeemed you, I have paid the ransom; come home."

Each of us has a story. For some of us the road home looked so long, so difficult, that it was years before we had the courage to start the journey. Some of us were so aware of how profoundly we had failed that it took the prophet many tellings before we could believe. Some of us may even be struggling this very hour, thinking that we have slipped beyond the reach of this message. But Yahweh says, "I even I, am the one who wipes out your transgressions for My own sake. And I will not remember your sins" (Isa. 43:25 NASB).

Yes, you are guilty. So am I. But the good news about sin is forgiveness, and the good news about God is that He forgives. Isaiah said: "Do not call to mind the former things, or ponder the things of the past. Behold I will do something new, now it will spring forth, will you not see it?" Indeed, the message of the gospel is that you and I are the new Israel. And just like the Israelites, we were guilty, we deserved His wrath; our *own* actions had driven us into exile. But in our exile we felt His grace, we believed the prophet, we took the step, and He traveled with us—home. Amazing grace, how sweet the sound.

So how does Isaiah 43 speak to the content of our calling as Christians? As we have seen, just like the Babylonian exiles, you and I have experienced the redemption of the Almighty. But also just like them, Yahweh has shown us His grace for a reason: "(in order that) this people whom I have designed for myself might recount my praise" (Isa. 43:21)!

Although our tendency is to view our experience of redemption as all about *us*, Isaiah tells us that you and I were restored so that we could serve as witnesses. In other words, this is not simply about *us*. Rather, our redemption is intended to serve as a beacon to the nations; what God has done for us, He can do for them. Jesus said that there are still many sheep who are not yet part of this fold. The truth is that thousands upon thousands of the sons of Adam and the daughters of Eve are still in Babylon; and even worse, like the "ten lost tribes" of the northern kingdom, many are forgotten, exiled somewhere beyond the reaches of memory and knowledge. These are still in exile. They have yet to hear the word of the prophet. They do not know that Yahweh has paid the ransom, that He has provided for their redemption, that He has given another in their place (Isa. 43:3–4). They have not heard that "I, even I, am the one who wipes out your transgressions for My own sake. And I will not remember your sins" (Isa. 43:25 NASB). They do not know that it is safe to come home.

> *Isaiah tells us that you and I were restored so that we could serve as witnesses.*

So to our amazement we see that this new thing about which Isaiah preached so long ago is ongoing. The story continues. The sons of Adam and the daughters of Eve must hear, for how can they believe unless they hear? As Isaiah said thousands of years ago to the biological sons of Abraham, so he says to those grafted in today: You have been shown the salvation of your God *so that* you could serve as witnesses to His glory. Tell them. Tell them that God is doing a new thing; tell them that it is safe to come home.

> *Amazing grace, how sweet the sound*
> *that saved a wretch like me.*
> *I once was lost, but now am found*
> *Was blind, but now I see.*
>
> —John Newton
> "Amazing Grace"

**NOTE**

1. Unless otherwise noted, Bible translations are the author's own.

# THE PRIZE OF THE
# HIGH CALLING OF GOD

*Maxie D. Dunnam*

NOT THAT I HAVE ALREADY OBTAINED ALL THIS, OR HAVE ALREADY BEEN MADE PERFECT, BUT I PRESS ON TO TAKE HOLD OF THAT FOR WHICH CHRIST JESUS TOOK HOLD OF ME. BROTHERS, I DO NOT CONSIDER MYSELF YET TO HAVE TAKEN HOLD OF IT. BUT ONE THING I DO: FORGETTING WHAT IS BEHIND AND STRAINING TOWARD WHAT IS AHEAD, I PRESS ON TOWARD THE GOAL TO WIN THE PRIZE FOR WHICH GOD HAS CALLED ME HEAVENWARD IN CHRIST JESUS. ALL OF US WHO ARE MATURE SHOULD TAKE SUCH A VIEW OF THINGS. AND IF ON SOME POINT YOU THINK DIFFERENTLY, THAT TOO GOD WILL MAKE CLEAR TO YOU. ONLY LET US LIVE UP TO WHAT WE HAVE ALREADY ATTAINED.

—PHIL. 3:12–16 (NIV)

The person who invented the bumper sticker was a genius. Millions of drivers are confronted with dozens of roving bulletin boards everyday as they approach the bumpers of cars in front of them. Religious folks have not missed this communication opportunity. We have the traditional messages, such as, "Honk if you love Jesus." A bit more whimsical one reads, "My boss is a Jewish carpenter." One humorous sticker warns, "In case of Rapture, this car will be unoccupied."

## Preferring Hell

As intrigued as I am, I have never put a bumper sticker on my car. But, I am tempted to start now. I'm thinking about printing my own sticker that reads, "MOST OF US PREFER THE HELL OF A PREDICTABLE SITUATION, RATHER THAN RISK THE JOY OF AN UNPREDICTABLE ONE."

This maxim is an ancient phenomenon. Remember God's call to Abraham: "Leave your country, your people and your father's household and go to the land I will show you" (Gen. 12:1 NIV). The writer of Hebrews recorded Abraham's response:

> By faith he made his home in the promised land like a stranger in a foreign country; he lived in tents, as did Isaac and Jacob, who were heirs with him of the same promise. For he was looking forward to the city with foundations, whose architect and builder is God. By faith Abraham, even though he was past age—and Sarah herself was barren—was enabled to become a father because he considered him faithful who had made the promise. And so from this one man, and he as good as dead, came descendants as numerous as the stars in the sky and as countless as the sand on the seashore. (Heb. 11:9–12 NIV)

Would I—would you—have followed God's call into a foreign land? Would we have responded faithfully? When we compare the stance of most of us to Abraham, the truth is obvious: Most of us prefer the hell of a predictable situation, rather than risk the joy of an unpredictable one.

Several pointed stories appear in Luke chapter 9. One of them records the time Jesus took Peter, James, and John up a mountain to pray. That intimate experience must have been ecstatic for those three disciples. A marvelous thing happened while they were praying: the appearance of Jesus' face changed and His clothes became dazzling white. Added to this epiphany was the sudden arrival of Moses and Elijah, who had conversation with Jesus.

Peter was relishing the experience and didn't want to give it up. He thought the presence of Jesus and the prophets could be bottled up and sustained in that place. "Master, it is good for us to be here. Let us put up three shelters—one for you, one for Moses and one for Elijah" (Luke 9:33). Luke adds this telling commentary to Peter's desire: "He did not know what he was saying."

A clear and persistent danger exists whenever we have ecstatic epiphany moments. These moments are rightly treasured in our hearts, just as the three disciples rejoiced in the transfiguration of Jesus with Moses and Elijah on the mountain. We are tempted, however, to perpetuate our mountaintop experiences so that we can enjoy them forever.

Similarly, sometimes we want to immortalize our Bible studies, churches, seminaries, or other Christian communities. These communities can be places where our broken hearts and wounded feelings have found healing. They can be places where our parched souls have been watered by gushing fresh water. They can be places where our lost faith has been found and our calling been made clear. A community may have challenged you to think and forced you to grow outside your comfort zone. The community may have been

*We often feel unprepared, ill-equipped, and afraid to step out of the comfort zone and into the unknown.*

a place where you were well equipped for a new yet unfamiliar ministry. The danger, however, is that our Christian communities can become our new, familiar yet narrow enclaves. The temptation is to close our groups off to the outside world so that we can enjoy them perpetually.

Even though our communities may have done their job of nurturing and equipping us to fulfill our vocations, we often feel unprepared, ill-equipped, and afraid to step out of the comfort zone and into the unknown. At these times we must admit—even confess—that we prefer the hell of a predictable situation, rather than risk the joy of an unpredictable one. It would be great to just stay in the moment, or at least stretch the experience out as long as we can by building a tabernacle on our mounts of transfiguration.

At points such as this, the Scripture of Philippians 3:12–16 comes to us. The core of this passage is Paul's confession and conviction: "Forgetting what is behind and straining toward what is ahead, I press on toward the goal to win the prize for which God has called me heavenward in Christ Jesus" (3:13–14 NIV).

## Know Who You Are

Paul is calling us to recognize *who* and *where* we are. Paul says, "Not that I have already obtained all this, or have already been made perfect, but I press on to take hold of that for which Christ Jesus took hold of me" (Phil. 3:12 NIV). He honestly locates himself before God and acknowledges who he is and where he is.

The Christian life is a journey, a process of growth in which we seek to "take hold" of the fullness of that which has been given us—"that for which Christ Jesus took hold of me," as Paul put it. We are Christian. That is, we are Christian by the profession of our faith and in our position in relation to the Lord who has accepted us. Now we must become what we are. We must bring the *condition* of our life into harmony with

*We must bring the condition of our life into harmony with our position.*

our *position.* We must work out our full salvation with fear and trembling in order to become the persons Jesus has called us to be.

An important part of this process is to recognize who and what we are. Kim (Dunnam) Reisman, my daughter, makes this point well. She has written a book, commissioned by The Upper Room, about how professional women (especially female pastors) balance all the demands of their lives (e.g., family, children, church, vocation). Her fourth chapter is entitled "The Search for Our Center: Discovering Who We Are." There she talks about one significant experience of her own self-discovery during a Walk to Emmaus event.

Throughout my life, I have lived somewhat in the shadow of my father, Maxie Dunnam . . . I have many reasons to feel fortunate to be Maxie Dunnam's daughter. Yet, that very phrase, "Maxie Dunnam's daughter," has also been a heavy burden. Just as Jesus' disciples saw "only Jesus," rather than the true person that God knew him to be, I have often wondered if people see the true person I really am—not Maxie's daughter, but Kim.

That question led me to take my husband's name when I married, bucking the practice of most of my friends to keep their maiden names. With a new name, I could control who knew my family connection and who didn't, and I could gain an opportunity to establish myself—*as myself*—beforehand.

Connected with the question of whether others saw the real me was the question of motive, "Do you really care about me because I'm me or do you just care about me because of who I'm related to?" When I was younger I thought I was being paranoid and overly sensitive, simply an insecure adolescent. But as I got older I realized I had good reason to be inquisitive. Shortly after moving to Lafayette I began receiving warm calls from colleagues welcoming me into the area, some even resulting in a meeting for lunch. Little did I know that word of my "secret" had gotten out. After a seemingly appropriate amount of time, several of my colleagues, who had been so interested in getting to know me, revealed the true source of their interest—my father's preaching schedule. "We would love to have him preach for us, would you ask him?" . . .

Then came Emmaus, my wonderful weekend of complete anonymity, not even being known as a clergy-person! What a remarkable experience of love—God's love transmitted through the love of others—for *me*. ME—the unique, unrepeatable miracle of God that I finally understood myself to be (even though I had been told I was that by my parents for longer than I could remember). KIM—not Maxie's daughter, not John's wife, not Nathan's or Maggie's or Hannah's mother, but Kim. It was as though a bright cloud had descended on me and I heard God's voice saying, "this is my beloved child." I knew who I was even if everyone else saw just Kim, or Maxie's daughter. The strangest part of this watershed weekend was that suddenly it didn't really matter whether or not anybody knew whose daughter I was. Suddenly it didn't even matter if there were people out there who might like me because of him rather than because of me. I knew who I was.

Not all of us have had to live in someone's shadow, yet the story of Jesus has meaning for each of us as we seek to discover who we are. God sees us and names us in ways that the world often fails to see. The person God sees is never mundane, never unacceptable. The person God sees is unique and loved from the start, arrayed in dazzling clothing and named as a child, a beloved child. As we look within ourselves in order to answer the question, "Who am I?" we must look not just at who we have been told we are by the world: a wife, a mother, a daughter, or simply a woman. We must look at who God believes us and desires us to be: someone with unique gifts, some discovered, some as yet unknown; someone loved and cared for—not because of what they *do*, or because of what they *are*—but simply *because* they *are*.[1]

I believe there are two frames of reference out of which we tend to operate as Christians, either of which is debilitating to our Christian growth and service. One is a false humility that refuses to name and claim our gifts. The second is a confidence that claims too much for ourselves and is not dependent enough upon the power of Christ.

In Philippians 3:12, Paul calls for balance between humility and overconfidence. Read this verse again: "Not that I have already obtained all this, or have already been made perfect, but I press on to take hold of that for which Christ Jesus took hold of me." We may be hesitant to make claims about where we are in our spiritual growth, but there should be no hesitation in our unshakable conviction and confidence that Christ Jesus has made us His own. We recognize who and where we are.

## Clinging and Crying

A second lesson from chapter 3 of Philippians is obvious and clearly stated: leave the past behind—"Forgetting what is behind and straining toward what is ahead, I press on" (vv. 3:13–14). The tense is present. I press on! This declaration is a shattering of that static, protective positioning of most of us—preferring the hell of a predictable situation, rather than risk the joy of an unpredictable one.

The talented motion picture director, Peter Bogdanovich, is well known for the genre of "nostalgic" movies. When he made *The Last Picture Show* and *Paper Moon*, someone asked him why he was attracted so much by the past. Mr. Bogdanovich said, "I like any time better than now. I just don't like what is happening today. The music bores me, the cars are ugly, the people are droll. So, I retreat to the past."

Bogdanovich is in good company—well, I'm not sure it is good company, but he is in a large company—because his stance is shared by so many people. They like any time better than now. It would be easy for any of us to fall into this trap of retreating into the past—often a mythical, idealized past. This trap is not too different from wanting to build a tabernacle on some mount of transfiguration.

We retreat in two ways. One is by clinging to the past in remembering the "good old days." There is nothing in such clinging that is even close to the Christian gospel. The gospel is about being a pilgrim people, people who dwell in tents because they are on a journey. Paul even referred to our bodies as tents, saying, "Here we have no permanent dwelling place." He talked about the earthly house of this tabernacle being dissolved and looking forward to a building of God, a house made not by human hands but an eternal dwelling in the heavens. So, to cling to the past is to miss all that the gospel is about.

Other people escape the present and retreat into the past by crying over it. They don't cling to it, but they mourn over it and thus live in it by nursing old grievances, rehearsing old regrets, and wallowing in guilt and shame about what has happened in the past.

Ms. Haversham, a character in Charles Dickens's *Great Expectations*, had been jilted by the only man she ever loved. She had received a letter from him, calling off their wedding while she was putting on her wedding dress for the ceremony. Something died inside her that day. She stopped all the clocks at twenty minutes before nine, the time the letter had arrived on her wedding day. She sealed up every window of the house. She never took off her wedding dress. There she sat, while her world wasted and withered away. There is a parable in Ms. Haversham: crying over the past, we stop the watches of our lives and bury ourselves in regret, grief, and guilt.

Either of these actions of clinging or crying drains us of vitality, blinds us to the magic of the present moment, and robs us of the wonder of living as God gives us the gift of life every day. A long time ago I saw a banner with words that have forever been lodged in my mind: "To live in joy is to live this 'now day' of resurrection." Remember the verse of the psalmist: "This is the day the LORD has made; let us rejoice and be glad in it" (Ps. 118:24 NIV). Recall the words of Jesus: "Therefore do not worry about tomorrow, for tomorrow will worry about itself. Each day has enough trouble of its own" (Matt. 6:34 NIV).

Leave the past behind you. Don't get buried in the hell of a predictable situation, rather than risk the joy of an unpredictable one.

## Taste My Jesus

The final lesson I want to address from the Philippians passage is this: Remember your proper subject. I purposefully put the lesson that way, rather than simply write, "Have a goal."

Part of the energy for living this "now day" of resurrection comes from the divine purpose in our life. So, Paul says, "I press on toward the goal to win the prize for which God has called me heavenward in Christ Jesus" (3:14 NIV). That kind of goal, an awareness of divine purpose and call, keeps us alive.

No one understood this insight better than Mother Teresa, who gave her life for the poorest of the poor. On one occasion she observed:

We all long for heaven where God is, but we have it in our power to be in heaven with him right now—to be happy with him now means: loving as he loves, helping as he helps, giving as he gives, serving as he serves, rescuing as he rescues, being with him twenty-four hours, touching him in his distressing disguise.[2]

Mother Teresa understood, as we must understand, that the prize of the high calling of God in Christ Jesus is not a prize that is to be ours in some far off tomorrow when the last

> *The high calling of God in Christ Jesus is a present reality energizing who we are and how we live.*

trumpet sounds and the angel calls us—though, to be sure, there is that reward of eternal life. Rather, the high calling of God in Christ Jesus is a present reality energizing who we are and how we live. If we would burn with the passion of the high calling of God in Christ Jesus— burn with the conviction that Christ Jesus has made us His own—then our Christian life would continue to grow, would expand, and would attract the kind of attention that would make a powerful witness wherever we are.

There is an apocryphal story about Paul Tillich which has circulated through e-mails. It's a false story, but it illustrates well the lesson at hand:

> The University of Chicago Divinity School each year hosts what is called "Baptist Day." It is an annual event when Baptists are invited to the school, because the school wants the Baptists' dollars to keep coming in. During lunch, the school has one of its greatest theological minds to present a lecture.

> One year Dr. Paul Tillich gave the address. Dr. Tillich spoke for two and one-half hours proving that the resurrection of Jesus was metaphorical, a faith proposition that was not literal reality. He quoted scholar after scholar and book after book. He concluded that since there was no such thing as the historical resurrection, the religious tradition of the church was groundless, emotional mumbo-jumbo. Christianity was based on a relationship with a risen Jesus who, in fact, never rose from the dead in any literal sense.

He then asked if there were any questions. After about thirty seconds, an old, African-American preacher with a head of short-cropped, woolly white hair stood up in the back of the auditorium. "Docta Tillich, I got one question," he said, as all eyes turned toward him. He reached into his sack lunch and pulled out an apple and began eating it. "Docta Tillich," . . . CRUNCH, MUNCH. "My question is a simple question," . . . CRUNCH, MUNCH . . . "Now, I ain't never read them books you read," . . . CRUNCH, MUNCH. "And, I can't recite the Scriptures in the original Greek," . . . CRUNCH, MUNCH. "I don't know nothin' about Niebuhr and Heidegger," . . . CRUNCH, MUNCH. He finished the apple. "All I wanna know is: This apple I just ate—was it bitter or sweet?"

Dr. Tillich paused for a moment and answered in exemplary scholarly fashion, "I cannot possibly answer that question, for I haven't tasted your apple."

The white-haired preacher dropped the core of his apple into his crumpled paper bag, looked up at Dr. Tillich, and said calmly, "Neither have you tasted my Jesus."

The 1,000 plus in attendance could not contain themselves. The auditorium erupted with applause and cheers. Dr. Tillich thanked his audience and promptly left the platform.[3]

The preacher's point is the bottom line. Have we tasted Jesus? Can the stance of Paul be ours? Let us learn to say with Paul, "Not that I have already obtained all this, or have already been made perfect, but I press on to take hold of that for which Christ Jesus took hold of me."

NOTES

1. Kimberly Dunnam Reisman, *The Christ-Centered Woman* (Nashville, Tenn.: Upper Room Books, 2000).

2. Peter Dwan, *Apostle of the Unwanted* (Melbourne, Australia: ACTS Publications, 1969).

3. As reported on www. truthorfiction.com/rumors/t/tillich.htm.

# THE TRANSFORMING POWER OF PURPOSE

*Steve G. W. Moore*

WHAT DOES THE LORD REQUIRE OF YOU? TO ACT JUSTLY AND
TO LOVE MERCY AND TO WALK HUMBLY WITH YOUR GOD.
—MICAH 6:8 (NIV)

Halfway through the four-second, 220-foot plunge into the fifty-degree water, John Kevin Hines had second thoughts. *I don't want to die, I want to live.* Fortunately, he lived to tell about it. "I was supposed to die," he said. "I wanted to die. But now every day since that jump I ask myself WHO *am I?* WHY *am I?*" Part of his newfound purpose is to tell others life is worth living. He wants to make sure others don't make the mistake he almost made of seeking "a permanent solution to a temporary problem."[1]

Who am I?

Whose am I?

What must I do?

These are three big questions that nearly all of us face and must respond to in different ways.

Do you remember that scene in *Forrest Gump* where Forrest finds out his mother is dying and he rushes to her bedside? She patiently and deliberately explains to Forrest that she is about to die and he will have to go on without her.

"But why, Mama, why?" Forrest asks.

She carefully explains she has an illness that will soon not let her go on.

Forrest is undeterred. He simply won't believe it. "But why, Mama, why?" he keeps asking.

"Because it is my destiny, Forrest," she replies.

Sensing this is more than an explanation, Forrest stops and asks, "And what is my destiny, Mama?"

"That is something each person must discover for themselves, Forrest," she counsels. "You have your own destiny, Forrest. It's just for you."[2]

Destiny . . . purpose . . . plan . . . calling. All words that strike both fear and excitement in our hearts. Excitement, because deep down we all desire to live our lives with a sense of being part of a purposeful plan, a destiny or calling. Fear, because we are worried about missing our destiny. Fear, because we wonder if God's calling for our lives could be something boring or, worse yet, something we downright detest.

George Bernard Shaw once remarked:

This is the true joy in life, the being used for a purpose recognized by yourself as a mighty one; the being thoroughly worn out before you are thrown on a scrap heap; the being a force of nature instead of a feverish selfish little clod of ailments and grievances complaining that the world will not devote itself to making you happy.[3]

We have a luxury few generations and cultures have had. For a good part of human history, men and women have struggled to secure warm shelter, regular food, and a safe environment. Even in our world today, that is how a significant number of our brothers and sisters live each day. But times are changing. Peter Drucker put it this way:

In a few hundred years, when the history of our time is written from a long term perspective, it is likely that the most important event those historians will see is not technology, not the Internet, not e-commerce. It is an unprecedented change in the human condition. For the first time—literally—substantial and rapidly growing numbers of people have choices. For the first time, they will have to manage themselves. And society is totally unprepared for that.[4]

The idea of thinking about "calling" and *choosing* what, where, and when one will work would not only amaze previous generations, it is but a distant hope for many of our day. So in one sense the idea of seeking our calling is both a luxury and an enormous responsibility.

On the other hand, calling is nothing new. Throughout the history of humankind, individuals and peoples have sought to live life with purpose and significance. I remember in college when I first encountered Victor Frankl's famous book *Man's Search for Meaning*. At first I was stunned, then perplexed, then amazed.

I was stunned at the story of one man's discovery of hope, purpose, and profound human value in the midst of a Nazi death camp. I was perplexed how humanity could ever deteriorate into such a state of chaos and disorder and destruction. (I later realized

> *Throughout the history of humankind, individuals and peoples have sought to live life with purpose and significance.*

it is the battle of every generation in one form or another). And, finally, I was amazed that more people aren't more stunned and perplexed and amazed at the lessons this book teaches us.

Frankl argues that human beings have a deep hunger for meaning—one that manifests itself in the myriad ways they pursue fulfillment. The principle lesson from the book is that not even a death camp can take away the joy and purposefulness that we can all hold inside our hearts.

Of course, the irony in our day is that we have so much freedom and yet are so unhappy in what we do! Researchers with the Harris Incentive Poll recently discovered that:

- Only 37 percent of the people have a clear understanding of what their work is about.
- Only 15 percent of people feel they are working in a trustworthy environment.
- Only 1 in 5 people feel good about what their job is trying to accomplish.[5]

This and other research has repeatedly shown that although we have the freedom to pursue meaning, far too often we do not do so. We often settle for too little, settle for trivial pursuits that distract us or give temporary pleasure but neither provide deep fulfillment nor contribute to the kingdom! Fortunately, we are wired in such a way that we are pulled, probed, prompted, and called to be a part of something bigger. Our hearts long to make a difference, to connect to something significant beyond ourselves.

> *We are wired in such a way that we are pulled, probed, prompted, and called to be a part of something bigger.*

It's like Frodo in *The Lord of the Rings* or Luke in *Star Wars*. We are compelled to leave the safe shire or the galactic sideline and get into the action—to become a part of a bigger story that has eternal significance.

## The Discovery Paradox

One might ask, "If there is something I am created or called to be, how do I find it?" A great question that has a surprise answer. While one must desire and seek one's vocation, you are already being sought out by God!

Perhaps you have heard of the young student C. S. Lewis, who discovered this truth in his young adult years as he traveled a journey from being a committed atheist to discovering God. Various life experiences began to seem to him as poignant, beyond just living life as a material being; they seemed to point to "something more." That's a feeling that many of us have experienced in a variety of ways in a wide

> *You are already being sought out by God.*

number of places. These various moments of realization Lewis describes as moments of being "surprised by joy." But, as Lewis came to realize, the experience of joy has no place in a naturalistic universe. Finally, unable to explain away these feelings, make sense of them, or deny them, Lewis began to see that the experiences were moments demonstrating the reality that God was pursuing and wooing him. "God closed in on me."[6] The seeker was found.

This leads us to ask, "Are you willing to be found?"

Another seeker who was found puts it this way, "Thou hast made us for thyself, O God, and our hearts are restless until they find their rest in thee."[7] God has built into our DNA a desire to know Him and be known by Him. The hunger for intimacy and purpose can be avoided—we can become experts at avoiding our call—but ultimately it *cannot* be escaped without significant consequences.

## Certainty and Faith

Invariably when conversations of vocation and calling take place, the question arises "How do you know for sure?" The short but unsatisfactory answer is: "You do and you don't." The longer answer requires two things that might, at first, seem to be out of place: other people and time.

Richard Bolles is someone whose calling has been to help zillions of other people discover their calling. He has written best-selling books like *What Color Is Your Parachute* and has led seminars around the world on finding one's calling.

In one of his books he challenges us to imagine ourselves walking one night when we are suddenly surrounded by dense fog and cannot find our way out. He goes on:

> Suddenly a friend appears out of the fog and asks you to put your hand in theirs, and they will lead you home. And you, not being able to tell where you are going, trustingly follow them, even though you can only see one step at a time. Eventually you arrive safely home, filled with gratitude. But as you reflect upon the experience the next day you realize how unsettling it was to have to keep walking when you could see only one step at a time, even though you had guidance in which you knew you could trust.[8]

This, Bolles suggests, is the essence of discovering our calling. Most of us imagine the discovery of our calling to be like going to a mountaintop, seeing a distant place, and being told "that is where you are going, that is where everything is leading, every step of your way."[9] But for most, that is not the way it happens at all. Instead we find ourselves in a fog.

Bolles goes on to say:

> And the voice in our ear says something quite different from what we thought we would hear. It says your mission is to take one step at a time, even when you don't see where it is

all leading, or what the Grand Plan is or what your overall mission in life is. Trust me, I will lead you.[10]

Part of the longer answer to discovering our calling is that relationships are the key to every calling. My friend Mike Peterson reminds us that any understanding of vocation needs to be rooted in our understanding of God as Trinity. The Trinity is relational—the three persons in one enjoying a joyful mutual existence. That is what is at the heart of all reality.[11]

*Because we are created in God's image, we too are relational beings.*

Because we are created in God's image, we too are relational beings. We are created for relationship with God—"to glorify Him and enjoy Him forever,"[12] as the Westminster Catechism puts it. But we are also called into relationship with others: our family, our friends, our spouse, our children, and the body of other believers, those in the world around us. We are wired for relationships, and those relationships help us see, hear, and understand our calling.[13]

And it is both in and through these relationships that our calling often unfolds. Healthy, vibrant relationships can often provide perspective, insight, and wisdom for us in our journey of discovering our call. Sometimes simply being in the midst of strong relationships, we are lifted up and see the needs of the world around us in a clearer, more personal way—needs that are calling to us. They may help us see opportunities that may utilize our unique gifting and personality so that we come fully alive.

Our relationship to God, relationships to others, even our relationship with our self are critical because we live in a relational universe. These relationships can also protect us from the great tragedy of hyper-individualism that so plagues Western

Christians. It keeps us from thinking vocation and calling are "I choose it for myself, by myself."

Throughout the centuries, followers of God have discerned their callings in the midst of a body of believers who love, forgive, advise, nourish, encourage, and ask. This is a key role of the body of Christians today. There is nothing to suggest that discovering our calling should be any different for those of us in the twenty-first century than it has been throughout the centuries before. Is it any surprise that a relational God in a relational creation would have it any other way?

Our calling in life is partly about understanding who we are (gifts, talents, energies, personality, etc.); partly understanding the varieties of needs in the world and the varieties of ways to address and meet those needs; and partly understanding who and how we relate to others. As each of those three understandings comes into focus, options narrow down and direction opens up that is a match with who you are. For most of us this doesn't happen all at once—it is a part of a process that takes time. That process isn't the way to life; it is in fact an important part of life!

I have come to understand that any and every time you or I forget that our character is one of God's central proposes for our lives, we will become frustrated by the circumstances of life. As James Buckman once observed:

> Trials, temptations, disappointments—all these are helps instead of hindrances, if one uses them rightly. They not only test the fiber of character but strengthen it. Every conquering temptation represents a newfound moral energy. Every trial endured and weathered in the right spirit makes a soul nobler and stronger than it was before.[14]

## Glorify or Enjoy

Dennis Hollinger tells of a student who once raised issue with the call to "Glorify God and enjoy Him forever." "My problem," the student observed, "is that I can never decide which it is I am really to be about—glorify or enjoy." She went on to describe her dilemma:

> To glorify God seems to imply that we should put controls on ourselves and our personal enjoyment in life. Glorifying God is to move beyond our own self interests to the interests of God . . . on the other hand enjoying God focuses on all the good things that God brings in Life. The enjoyment of God seems to end up inadvertently focusing on ourselves as we celebrate the blessings and gifts of God, and in turn this enjoyment appears contrary to the pursuit of God's glory.[15]

Hollinger points the student in the direction of the Psalms which remind us that life is about rhythm and balance, not simplistic formulaic answers. Psalm 67, for example, is one text that models for us the powerful energy and dynamic that occurs when glorifying God and enjoying His creation are held together. "May God be gracious to us and bless us and make his face to shine upon us" of verse 1 echoes the much older blessing found in the book of Numbers: "The Lord bless you and keep you; the Lord make his face to shine upon you, and be gracious to you; the Lord life up his countenance upon you, and give you peace" (Num. 6:24–26 RSV).

*Life is about rhythm and balance, not simplistic formulaic answers.*

From their very beginning, the people of Israel realized that all good things ultimately come from God. He desires to bless our lives and for us to be a blessing to the world in which we live. Jesus was echoing this promise when He proclaimed, "I

have come that you might have life and have it abundantly"
(John 10:10 RSV).

That is why in verse 2 of Psalm 67, we are reminded of the
goal of God's blessing: "That your way may be known upon earth,
your saving power among all the people of the earth." Hollinger
goes on to reflect on the Psalm this way:

> The Psalmist certainly wants to enjoy the blessing of God. They
> are wonderful gifts that remind us that God is a self-giving God
> of grace and mercy. We follow a God who wants the very best
> for us in life and desires that we experience joy, peace, hope,
> meaning, and a sense of divine presence and power within. But
> it is equally clear that we cannot stop there, for the enjoyment
> of God is not for our own self-centeredness. It is a true enjoy-
> ment, but never narcissistic. It is true pleasure, but never
> pleasure as an end in itself apart from wider context, purpose,
> and meaning.[16]

I remember once being told that pursuing our calling is like
keeping a conversation going through our lives, regularly asking,
"Now God, what might you have me to do?" And we must trust
that one of the measures of being where we should be is when we
sense a certain "aliveness" in our lives. This is not a flaky, goose-
bumpy aliveness. It is an aliveness that is a deep sense that all of
who I am is being engaged and deployed to make a difference in
the lives of people around me and in the world in which we live.

## Don't Be Too Happy

A friend of mine battles what I call "the-other-shoe
syndrome." He grew up in an environment where anytime you
got too happy, or feeling too good about things, he was told to
expect God to bring something bad into his life. "I was always
waiting or the other shoe to drop," he would say. The under-
lying belief was that God didn't want you to be too happy. If
you were feeling too good, you needed to be brought back

"down to earth" so you'd depend on Him. Sort of a classic killjoy or celestial sourpuss.

John Fisher had a similar experience:

> I grew up with a kind of warped Christianity that taught that if I was passionate about something, it was probably wrong. God was the great killjoy in the sky. Virtue was painful. The good usually felt bad. The bad (we were told) felt good. Denying yourself meant never doing anything you really wanted to do. Conversely, if you hated doing something that most likely was what God was calling you to do. "God, please don't send me to Africa" was a prayer you'd better not pray, because that was the first place he would probably send you if you prayed that prayer. As you might imagine, this kind of thinking turned out a generation of very dull, boring Christians who were always suspicious of having fun.[17]

Of course the greatest danger of all is not that you get paralyzed by some fear of being too happy. Nor is the greatest danger that you pursue wild tangents on a quest to serve God. The greatest danger is that you do nothing. Our deepest sadness should be reserved for those who simply settle into a safe, dull routine. They go through the motions every day helping no one, harming no one, mindlessly plodding through, occasionally entertained.

Edmund Burke's now famous quote should be over every person's doorpost, "All that is necessary for the forces of evil to win in this world is for enough good people to do nothing."[18]

Truth be told, we are at war. We are a part of two worlds at once. A battle is occurring for the heart of humankind and the heart of every person you know. We must not underestimate our role, the crucial part we play in this battle. Every person counts; no one can go it alone.

But there is one thing that no one can do for you. Choose. Step out. Act on what you know.

Mark Twain is reported to have once observed, "My problem is not with the parts of the Bible I don't understand. My challenge is doing what the parts of the Bible I do understand tell me to do!"[19]

God is calling. Take that first step, then the next to be and do who and what you were created to be and do. It's worth it. And the truth is, there is no other way.

NOTES

1. Staff, "A Jump Survivor's Bridge to Activism," *Los Angeles Times* (May 23, 2005): A1.

2. *Forrest Gump*, Paramount Studios, 1994.

3. George Bernard Shaw, *"Man and Superman": A Comedy and a Philosophy* (London: Penguin Books, 1941), 26.

4. Peter Drucker, "Managing Knowledge Means Managing Ourselves," *Leader to Leader* 16 (spring 2000): 8–10.

5. Stephen Covey, Harris Interactive Poll as quoted in *The Eighth Habit* (New York: Free Press, 2004), 2.

6. C. S. Lewis, *Surprised by Joy* (Orlando, Fla.: Harcourt Brace, 1955), 216.

7. Augustine, *Confessions* (New York: Oxford University Press, 1992), 3.

8. Richard Bolles, *How to Find Your Mission in Life* (Berkeley, Calif.: Ten Speed Press, 2000), 36–37.

9. Ibid.

10. Ibid.

11. Mike Peterson, unpublished chapel address, Asbury College (Feb. 9, 2005).

12. Douglas F. Kelly, *The Westminster Confession of Faith: An Authentic Modern Version* (Signal Mountain, Tenn.: Summertown Texts, 1992).

13. Peterson, Chapel Address.

14. James Buckman, www.powerfulquotes.com, 2/26/99.

15. Dennis Hollinger, "To Glorify or Enjoy Forever," *C. S. Lewis Institute Newsletter*, (summer 2003): 3.

16. Ibid.

17. John Fischer, "God Don't Send Me to Africa," *Purpose Driven Daily Devotional* (May 11, 2005): 1.

18. Edmund Burke, *A Philosophical Enquiry* (Oxford: Oxford University Press, 1956), 96.

19. Howard Baetzhold and Joseph McCullough, *The Bible According to Mark Twain* (New York: Touchstone with University of Georgia Press, 1996), 46.

# BIBLIOGRAPHY

Augsburger, Myron. *The Communicator's Commentary: Matthew.* Lloyd Ogilvie, ed. Waco, Tex.: Word Books, 1982.

Barclay, William. *The Gospel of John: Vol. 2.* New York: Hyperion Books, 1993.

Bartlett, Robert Merrill. *The Pilgrim Way.* Philadelphia: Pilgrim Press, 1971.

Blackaby, Henry and Claude King. *Experiencing God: Knowing and Doing the Will of God.* Nashville, Tenn.: Lifeway Press, 1990.

*Book of Discipline of the United Methodist Church.* Nashville, Tenn.: United Methodist Publishing House, 1996.

Borgman, Paul. *Genesis: The Story We Haven't Heard.* Downers Grove, Ill.: InterVarsity Press, 2001.

Brother Lawrence. *The Practice of the Presence of God: Brother Lawrence.* New Kensington, Pa.: Whitaler House, 1982.

"Down the Rabbit Hole," *The Matrix* DVD, directed by Andy and Larry Wachowski (Burbank, Calif.: Warner Bros. Home Video, 1999).

*Encyclopedia Americana*, s.v. "Wilberforce."

Friesen, Garry and J. Robin Maxson. *Decision Making and the Will of God: A Biblical Alternative to the Traditional View.* Sisters, Ore.: Multnomah, 1985.

Garber, Steve. *The Fabric of Faithfulness: Weaving Together Belief and Behavior during the University Years.* Downers Grove, Ill.: InterVarsity Press, 1996.

Giglio, Louie. Unpublished sermon notes. Asbury Theological Seminary, April 2003.

Gonzales-Balado, Jose Luis. *Mother Teresa: In My Own Words.* New York: Random House, 1996.

Guinness, Os. *Doubt.* Downers Grove, Ill.: InterVarsity Press, 1976.

———. *The Call.* Nashville, Tenn.: W Publishing Group, 1998, 2003.

Hammarskjold, Dag. *Markings.* New York: Ballantine Books, 1964.

Hardy, Lee. *Fabric of This World.* Grand Rapids, Mich.: Eerdmans, 1990.

Hutchinson, Courtney. *The Book of Common Prayer.* New York: Henry Holt & Co., 1992.

Kidd, Sue Monk. *When the Heart Waits: Spiritual Direction for Life's Sacred Questions.* New York: HarperCollins, 1990.

Kinlaw, Dennis. "A Hunger for Holiness," *A Vision for Holiness*, tape 1. Wilmore, Ky.: Francis Asbury Society, 1991.

Mowat, Don. Unpublished remarks. Asbury Seminary, January 2004.

Outler, Albert and Richard Heitzenreter, eds. *John Wesley's Sermon: An Anthology.* Nashville, Tenn.: Abingdon Press, 1991.

Palmer, Parker. *The Courage to Teach.* San Francisco: Jossey-Bass, 1998.

Reisman, Kim Dunnam. *The Christ-Centered Woman.* Nashville, Tenn.: Upper Room Books, 2000.

Roazen, Paul. *Erik H. Erikson: The Power & Love of a Vision.* New York, N.Y.: Free Press, 1976.

Sine, Tom. *Mustard Seed Versus McWorld.* Grand Rapids, Mich.: Baker, 1999.

Sittser, Gerald. *The Will of God As a Way of Life.* Grand Rapids, Mich.: Zondervan, 2000.

Smith, Gordon T. *Alone with the Lord: A Guide to a Personal Day of Prayer.* Vancouver, B.C.: Regent College Publishing, 2003.

Stone, Lawson. *Unpublished lecture notes.* N.p., 2004.

Stott, John. *The Essential John Stott: A Double Volume for a New Millennium*. Downers Grove, Ill.: InterVarsity Press, 1999.

Sweazey, George E. *Effective Evangelism*. New York: Harper & Brothers, 1953.

Taylor, Herbert J. *The Herbert J. Taylor Story*. Downers Grove, Ill.: InterVarsity Press, 1968.

Tolkien, J. R. R. *The Lord of the Rings*. New York: Random House, 1981.

*United Methodist Hymnal*. Nashville, Tenn.: United Methodist Publishing House, 1989.

Vaughan, David. *Statesman and Saint: The Principled Politics of William Wilberforce* Nashville, Tenn.: Cumberland House, 2002.

Walsh, Brian and J. R. Middleton. *The Transforming Vision: Shaping a Christian World View*. Downers Grove, Ill.: InterVarsity Press, 1984.

Wangerin, Walter, Jr. *As for Me and My House: Crafting Your Marriage to Last*. Nashville, Tenn.: Thomas Nelson Publishers, 1987.

Wesley, John. *The Journal of John Wesley*. Chicago: Moody Press, 1974.

Yancey, Philip. *The Jesus I Never Knew*. Grand Rapids, Mich.: Zondervan, 1995.